INVESTING

PRAISE FOR

INVESTING

"[*Investing*] is the road map for a fabulous intellectual journey, with wisdom and insight around every corner. Read this book and live its message. Your investment performance and your mind will thank you."
— Michael J. Mauboussin, Chief U.S. Investment Strategist, Credit Suisse First Boston

"[*Investing*] is a different investment book. It contains no math and provides a web, rather, 'lattice,' in which to climb around and explore complexity. Markets are archetypical complex adaptive systems and Hagstrom's book is among the first to study them using a new science." — Dean LeBaron, Chairman, Virtualquest.company and Trustee, Santa Fe Institute

"Any investor who doesn't come away from [*Investing*] with some new ideas simply isn't human."
— Kenneth Fisher, "Portfolio Strategy" Columnist, *Forbes* and CEO, Fisher Investments, Inc.

"Over the weekend, I read a book that reminded me why I love investing. You should read it too. The book is called *Investing: The Last Liberal Art. Investing* . . . is a thrilling intellectual exercise that rewards thoroughness, creativity, and a willingness to stick your neck out and go against the grain. Kudos to Robert Hagstrom for reminding us of this." — Pat Dorsey, Morningstar.com

"*Investing* seduces the reader with the sheer simplicity of its biological and psychological metaphors." —*Business 2.0*

"*Investing: The Last Liberal Art* is an elegant and irresistible book. — James Surowiecki, *The New Yorker*

INVESTING

The Last Liberal Art

ROBERT G. HAGSTROM

TEXERE

NEW YORK • LONDON

Published in 2000 by

TEXERE LLC
55 East 52nd Street
New York, New York 10055

Tel: +1(212) 317-5511
Fax: +1 (212) 317-5178
www.extexe.com

In the U.K.

TEXERE Publishing Limited
71–77 Leadenhall Street
London EC3A 3DE

Tel: +44 (0)20 7204 3644
Fax: +44 (0)20 7208 6701
www.etexere.co.uk

ISBN 1-58799-000-8 (hc)
ISBN 1-58799-138-1 (pb)

Printed in the United States of America

This book is printed on acid-free paper.

10 9 8 7 6 5 4 3 2 1

To Bill Miller

TEACHER, COLLEAGUE, AND FRIEND

PREFACE

Let me start with a loud disclaimer: This is not a how-to book on investing. It does not provide a new set of step-by-step instructions on how to pick stocks or manage your portfolio. However, after reading the book, what you will have, if you are willing to spend some time with challenging ideas, is a new way to *think* about investing and a clearer understanding of how markets and economies work. It is an understanding derived not from the economic and finance textbooks, but from the basic truths embedded in a number of seemingly unrelated disciplines, including physics, biology, the social sciences, psychology, philosophy, and literature.

To develop this new understanding, you and I will walk together through those areas of knowledge, investigating the basic and fundamental concepts from each field. Sometimes we will begin with a historical overview to see how the concepts originated and then move forward; always we shall examine how those concepts relate to investing and the markets. One chapter at a time, one piece at a time, with some of the greatest minds of all time, we shall assemble a new and original way to think about investing.

I must confess that writing this book was difficult. It required me to delve deeply into several different disciplines and then distill the essence of each into one short chapter. The discussions are, of necessity and without undue apology, both brief and general. If you happen to be an expert in any one of these disciplines, you may quibble with my presentation or may conclude I have omitted certain concepts. However, I hope you appreciate that to do otherwise would have resulted in a book with chapters one hundred pages long and a final manuscript equal in proportion to an encyclopedia. While writing this book I came to believe it was far more important to deliver an abbreviated sermon to a larger number of people than restrict its overall message to the few who would be willing to tackle a dissertation. For this reason, I hope you will recognize it was necessary to limit the descriptions in each discipline to the very basics.

Even so, many readers may find that reading this book is something of a challenge, no less than the writing of it was for me. It is challenging on two levels. First, some of the chapters may deal with disciplines that are unfamiliar to you, and reading them may remind you of an intensive college-level seminar. Nonetheless, it is my hope that you will find the exposure to new ideas a stimulating and rewarding experience. Second, because each chapter presents a completely different field of study, the total benefit of the book may not be fully clear until you reach the end. It is a cumulative process, with each chapter adding a new layer of ideas. I have tried to point out common themes and mental links, but my comments are no substitute for your own personal revelation that will come from a careful study and thoughtful reflection.

Reading this book requires, then, both an intellectual curiosity and a significant measure of patience. In a world that increasingly seeks to solve our needs in the shortest amount of time, this book may be an anomaly. However, I have always believed there are no easy shortcuts to greater understanding. You simply have to work through the basics.

ONE THING THAT HISTORY TEACHES US is that no great idea ever originated in a vacuum, arriving whole and complete in the mind of man in one instant flash. Rather, each thought, each discovery, each invention, builds on countless earlier ideas and in turn triggers many others. That is how society advances. The idea for this book followed a similar path.

Like most investment professionals, I began my career with a systematic study of accounting, economics, and finance. Armed with this knowledge, I set forth to help my clients prosper. But despite reading huge stacks of books, magazines, journals, and research reports, oftentimes I felt the information I garnered from them was inadequate. Over the years, it became more and more obvious that what I observed and experienced in the market was not fully explained by the canons of the investment industry.

Gradually I sought out the best minds in our industry, with the hope that I could learn their basic lessons and in turn achieve success. This journey led me to studying and writing about one of the greatest investors ever—Warren Buffett. It was through Warren that I eventually learned about his exceptional partner, Charlie Munger. A highly successful investor himself, Charlie continually preached the need for a liberal arts understanding of investing. Achieving worldly wisdom by building a latticework of mental models, said Charlie, would greatly help people in their pursuit of higher investment returns. Although I recognized the value of Charlie's theory of mental models, it remained just that—a theory—until I developed a closer friendship with Bill Miller.

Bill is president of Legg Mason Funds Management and portfolio manager of the Legg Mason Value Trust. Bill is, without question, the most talented and successful portfolio manager in the market. He is the only manager who beat the Standard & Poor's 500-stock index every year from 1991 to 1999. He was Morningstar's Domestic Equity Manager of the Year in 1998, and the following year, 1999, the analysts at Morningstar voted him the Domestic Equity Manager of the Decade. Bill, like most of us, started in the business studying the finance basics. He also added a careful study of the other great investors, including Benjamin Graham and Warren Buffett. But he also did something extra, something I now believe is largely responsible for his success.

Bill Miller did not confine his education within the fences of our investment industry. It is not even accurate to say that he peeked over the fence at other disciplines. With energy and passion, he *charged* over those fences, engaging himself in a careful study of physics, biology, philosophy, and psychology. He then worked to connect the lessons he learned in other disciplines back to the investment world.

This broad-based approach is the heart of the New Investing. It is no longer enough just to acquire and master the basics in accounting, economics, and finance. To generate above-average returns, I believe, requires much more. The New Investing theorized by Charlie Munger and practiced by Bill Miller starts with the basics and then extends outward in all directions, toward any and all disciplines. It is driven by a keen mental appetite to discover and use new insights regardless of what Dewey decimal number they bear or how unrelated they may at first appear.

Now let's be clear. Will reading this book ensure that you generate the same investment results as Bill Miller? No. The smarter question is whether reading this book will help you earn better investment results than you have achieved in the past. I believe that answer is yes. Mistakes in investing most often occur because of investor confusion. In my opinion, the basic investment lessons we have learned thus far have not given us a complete view of how markets work. No wonder we're confused. No wonder we make mistakes. When we don't understand something, there is always a fifty-fifty chance we will make the wrong decision. If this book improves, even slightly, your understanding of investing and how markets work, then the odds of success will tilt in your favor.

ROBERT G. HAGSTROM
Wayne, Pennsylvania
July 2000

CONTENTS

INVESTING

CHAPTER 1

A LATTICEWORK OF
MENTAL MODELS

I n April 1994, at the Marshall School of Business of the University of Southern California, students in Dr. Guilford Babcock's Student Investment Seminar got a rare treat: a powerful dose of real-world knowledge from a man whose thoughts on money are widely considered priceless.

Charles Munger—Charlie, as he is known throughout the investment world—is vice chairman of Berkshire Hathaway, the holding company run by Warren Buffett, the world's most famous investor. Trained originally as an attorney, Charlie is Buffett's partner, friend, and straight man. He commands attention whenever he speaks.

Charlie Munger is an intellectual jewel somewhat hidden behind his more celebrated partner. This anonymity is not Warren's fault. Charlie simply prefers the lower profile. Except for specific appearances such as the one at USC and his prominent role at Berkshire Hathaway's annual meetings, he remains largely out of public view. Even at those annual meetings, he deliberately keeps his remarks brief, allowing Buffett to answer most of the questions from shareholders. But occasionally Charlie does have something to add, and when he speaks, the shareholders straighten and shift forward to the edge of their seats, straining to get a better view, to catch every word.

In Dr. Babcock's classroom that day in April, the atmosphere was much the same. The students knew whom they were listening to, and they were anticipating receiving the benefit of considerable investment expertise. What they got instead was something infinitely more valuable.

At the outset, Charlie mischievously admitted that he was about to play something of a trick on his audience. Rather than discussing the stock market, he intended to talk about "stock picking as a subdivision of the art of worldly wisdom."[1] For the next hour and a half, he challenged the students to broaden their vision of the market, of finance, and of economics in general; to see them not as separate disciplines but as part of a larger body of knowledge, one that also incorporates psychology, engineering, mathematics, physics, and the humanities.

In this broader view, he suggested, each discipline entwines with, and in the process strengthens, every other. From each discipline the thoughtful person draws significant mental models, the key ideas that combine to produce a cohesive understanding. Those who cultivate this broad view are well on their way to achieving worldly wisdom, that solid mental foundation without which success in the market—or anywhere else—is merely a short-lived fluke.

To drive his point home, Charlie used a memorable metaphor to describe this interlocking structure of ideas: a latticework of models. "You've got to have models in your head," he explained, "and you've got to array your experience—both vicarious and direct—on this latticework of models." So immediate is this visual image that *latticework* has become something of a shorthand term in the investment world, a quick and easily recognized reference to Munger's approach.

It is a theme he returns to often. At the Berkshire Hathaway annual meetings, for instance, he frequently adds to Buffett's answer to a question by quoting from a book he has recently read. Often the quote at first appears to have no direct link to investing, but with Charlie's explanation it quickly becomes relevant. It is not that Warren's answers are incomplete. Far from it. It is just that when Charlie is able to connect Warren's ideas to similar ideas in other disciplines, it tends to elevate the level of understanding among the group.

Charlie's attention to other disciplines is purposeful. He operates in the firm belief that uniting the mental models from separate disciplines in such a way as to create a latticework of understanding is a powerful way to achieve superior investment results. Investment decisions are more likely to be correct when ideas from other disciplines lead to the same conclusions. That is the topmost payoff—broader understanding makes us better investors. It will be immediately obvious, however, that the ramifications are much wider. Those who strive to understand connections are well on the way to worldly wisdom. This makes us not only better investors but better leaders, better citizens, better parents, spouses, and friends.

How does one achieve worldly wisdom? To state the matter concisely, it is an ongoing process of, first, acquiring the significant concepts—the models—from many areas of knowledge and then, second, learning to recognize patterns of similarity among them. The first is a matter of educating yourself; the second is a matter of learning to think and see differently.

Acquiring the knowledge of many disciplines may seem a daunting task. Fortunately, you don't have to become an expert in every field. You merely have to learn the fundamental principles—what Charlie calls the big ideas—and learn them so well that they are always with you. The following chapters of this book are intended as a starting point for this self-education. Each one examines a specific discipline—physics, biology, social sciences, psychology, philosophy, and literature—from the perspective of its contribution to a latticework of models. Of course many other sources are available to the intellectual explorer.

A protest is commonly heard at this point: isn't that what a college education is supposed to do for us, teach us the critical concepts that have been developed over the centuries? Of course. Most educators will tell you, in passionate terms, that a broad curriculum grounded in the liberal arts is the best way, perhaps the only way, to produce well-educated people. Few would argue with that position in theory. But in reality we have become a society that prefers specialization over breadth.

This is wholly understandable. Because students and parents spend a small fortune on a college education, they expect this investment to pay off promptly, in the form of good job offers after graduation. They know that most corporate recruiters want workers with specialized knowledge, who can make an immediate and specific contribution to the organization. It is little wonder that most of today's students, faced with this pressure, resist a broad, liberal arts education in favor of a specialty major.

At one point in our history, we were given a superb model of what constitutes a good education. Perhaps we should have paid better attention.

• ■ •

IN THE SUMMER OF 1749, subscribers to the *Pennsylvania Gazette* received, along with their newspaper, an additional pamphlet written by the newspaper's publisher, Benjamin Franklin. He described this pamphlet, entitled *Proposals Relating to the Education of Youth in Pensilvania,* as a "Paper of Hints" to address the regret that the "youth of the Province had no academy."[2] The young men in Connecticut and Massachusetts were already attending Yale and Harvard, Virginians had the College of William and Mary, and students in New Jersey were served by the College of New Jersey (later called Princeton). But Philadelphia, the largest and richest city in the Colonies, known as the Athens of America, had no institution of higher learning. In his pamphlet Franklin explained his proposal to remedy that, with the establishment of the Public Academy of Philadelphia.

Franklin's concept was unique for its day. Harvard, Yale, Princeton, and William and Mary were schools for educating the clergy; their curricula stressed classical studies rather than the practical lessons that prepared young men for business and public service. It was Franklin's hope the Philadelphia Academy would stress both the traditional classical areas (which he termed "ornamental") as well as the practical. "As to their studies," he wrote, "it would be well if they could be taught everything that is useful and everything that is ornamental. But art is long and their time is short. It is therefore proposed that they learn those things that are likely to be most useful and most ornamental, regard being had to the several professions for which they are intended."

Today Franklin's Public Academy of Philadelphia is the University of Pennsylvania. The dean of its College of Arts and Sciences, Dr. Richard Beeman, describes the scope of Franklin's achievement.[3] "Benjamin Franklin proposed the first modern-day secular curriculum," he explains, "and the timing was perfect." In the eighteenth century the world's knowledge base was exploding with new discoveries in mathematics and the sciences, and the classical curriculum of Greek, Latin, and the Bible was no longer sufficient to explain this new knowledge. Franklin proposed including these new areas in the academy, and then he went further still: he also recommended that students acquire the necessary skill sets to become successful in business and public service, which then included writing, drawing, speaking, and arithmetic. Once students mastered the basic skills, said Franklin, then they could devote attention to acquiring knowledge.

"Almost all kinds of useful knowledge would be learned through the reading of history," wrote Franklin. But he meant much more than the definition we customarily attach to a history discipline; for Franklin, "history" encompassed all that is meaningful and worthwhile. By encouraging young men to read history, Franklin meant them to learn philosophy, logic, mathematics, religion, government, law, chemistry, biology, health, agriculture, physics, and foreign languages. To those who wondered whether such a burdensome task were really necessary, Franklin replied that it was not a burden to learn, but a gift. If you read the universal histories, he said, "it would give you a connected idea of human affairs."

"Benjamin Franklin was the originator of a liberal arts education," Beeman points out. "He was in the business of cultivating habits of mind. The Philadelphia Academy was a broadly based platform for lifelong learning. Of course Franklin is the perfect role model. He kept his mind open and his intellectual ambition fully fueled. As an educator he is my hero."

Beeman continues: "Benjamin Franklin's success as an educator was based upon three standing principles. First the student must acquire the basic skill sets: reading, writing, arithmetic, physical education, and public speaking. Then the student was introduced to the bodies of knowledge, and finally the student was taught to cultivate habits of mind by discovering the connections that exist between the bodies of knowledge."

IN THE 250 YEARS SINCE Franklin's proposal, American educators have continued to debate the best method to train young minds, and college administrators have continued to adjust their curricula in hope of attracting the best students. Critics of our current education system remain, and many of their criticisms seem valid, yet for all its faults, our education system today has done a reasonably good job of providing skills and producing knowledge—the first two of Franklin's key principles. What is often lacking is his third principle: the "habits of mind" that seek to link together different bodies of knowledge.

We can change this. Even if our days of formal schooling are behind us, we can search on our own for the linkages between ideas in various arenas, the connections that illuminate real understanding.

• ■ •

IT IS OF COURSE EASY to see that cultivating Franklin's "habits of mind," to use Professor Beeman's wonderful phrase, is the key to achieving Charlie Munger's "worldly wisdom." But seeing this is one thing; acting on it is another. For many of us, this goes against the mental grain. After having invested many years in learning one specialty, we are now being asked to teach ourselves others. We are told not to be bound by the narrow confines of the discipline we were trained in, but to leap over the intellectual fences and look at what's on the other side.

For investors, the rewards for making the effort are enormous. When you allow yourself to look beyond the immediate fences, you are able to observe similarities in other fields and recognize patterns of ideas. Then, as one concept is reinforced by another and another and then another, you know you are on the right track. The key is finding the linkages that connect one idea to another. Fortunately for us, the human mind already works this way.

● ■ ●

IN 1895, a young graduate student named Edward Thorndike began to study animal behavior under the psychologist and philosopher William James at Harvard University. We shall meet Mr. James later in this book, in another capacity; for now our interest in Thorndike is his groundbreaking research in how learning takes place, in humans as well as in animals. Thorndike was the first to develop what we now recognize as the stimulus-response framework, in which learning occurs when associations—connections—are formed between stimuli and responses.

Thorndike continued his studies at Columbia University, where he worked closely with Robert S. Woodworth. Together they investigated the process by which learning is transferred. They concluded, in a paper published in 1901, that learning in one area does not facilitate learning in other areas; rather, they argued, learning is transferred only when both the original and the new situations have similar elements. That is, if we understand A, and recognize something in B that resembles A, then we are well on the way to understanding B. In this view, learning new concepts has less to do with a change in a person's learning ability than with the existence of commonalities. We do not learn new subjects because we have somehow become better learners, but because we have become better at recognizing patterns.

EDWARD THORNDIKE'S THEORY of learning lies at the core of the contemporary theory in cognitive science called "connectionism." (The cognitive sciences encompass how the brain works—how we think, learn, reason, remember, and make decisions.) Connectionism, building from Thorndike's studies of stimulus-response patterns, holds that learning is a process of trial and error in which favorable responses to new situations (stimuli) actually alter the neural connections between brain cells. That is, the process of learning affects the synaptical connections between neurons, which are continually adjusting as they recognize familiar patterns and accommodate new information. The brain has the ability to link together related connections into a chain and to transfer what was learned to similar situations; intelligence, therefore, can be viewed as a function of how many connections a person has learned.

Connectionism has received a great deal of recent attention from business leaders as well as scientists because it is at the heart of a powerful new system of information technology known as "artificial neural networks." These neural networks, as they are more commonly called, attempt to replicate the workings of the brain more closely than has been possible with traditional computers.

In the brain, neurons function within groups called networks, each with thousands of interconnected neurons. We can therefore think of the brain as a collection of neural networks. Artificial neural networks, in turn, are computers that mimic the basic structure of the brain: they consist of hundreds of processing units (analogous to neurons) that are crossconnected into a complex network. (Surprisingly, neurons are several orders of magnitude slower than silicon chips, but the brain makes up for this lack of speed by having a massive number of connections that afford enormous efficiencies.)

The great power of a neural network, and the quality that sets it apart from a traditional computer, is that the weighting of the connections between its units can be adjusted, just as the brain's synapses adjust, becoming weaker or stronger, or even rewired altogether, as needed to perform different tasks. A neural network can learn. Just like the human brain, it has the ability to recognize complex patterns, classify new information into patterns, and draw associations between new data.

We are only beginning to understand how this technology can be applied in the business world. A few examples: A manufacturer of baby foods uses the technology to manage trading of cattle futures. Soft drink bottlers use it as an "electronic nose" to catch and analyze unpleasant odors. Credit card companies use it to detect forged signatures and to spot fraud by identifying deviations in spending habits. Mortgage underwriters use it to forecast creditworthiness. Many manufacturers of food products use it in quality control. Airlines use it to forecast flight demand, and one airline relies on it to determine which soft drinks its passengers are most likely to request. Postal services use neural networks to decipher sloppy handwriting, weather services use them for forecasting, and computer companies use them to develop software that will recognize handwritten notes for fax transmission and engineering schematics sketched on a cocktail napkin.

● ■ ●

THE PROCESS OF BUILDING and using a latticework of mental models is an innovative approach to thinking, and one that can seem intimidating to many laypeople, to the point of mental paralysis. Fortunately, there is a road map to the process that is easy to understand and to follow.

The Santa Fe Institute, in Santa Fe, New Mexico, is a multidisciplinary research and education facility where physicists, biologists, mathematicians, computer scientists, psychologists, and economists gather to study complex systems. These scientists are attempting to understand and predict immune systems, central nervous systems, ecologies, and economies, and they are all keenly interested in new ways of thinking.

John H. Holland, a professor in two fields at the University of Michigan—psychology, and engineering and computer science—is a frequent visitor to the Santa Fe Institute, where he has lectured extensively on innovative thinking. According to Holland, innovative thinking requires us to master two important steps. First, we must understand the basic disciplines from which we are going to draw knowledge; second, we need to be aware of the use and benefit of metaphors.

You will recognize the first step as being exactly the same as the first part of Charlie Munger's process for acquiring worldly wisdom. The ability to link mental models together and then benefit from the connections assumes that you have a basic understanding of each model in the latticework. There is no benefit to stringing mental models together if you have no idea how each model works and what phenomena it describes. Remember, though, it is not necessary to become an expert in each model, but merely to understand the fundamentals.

The second step—finding metaphors—may at first seem surprising, especially if it makes you think of your ninth-grade English class. At the simplest level, a metaphor is a way to convey meaning using out-of-the-ordinary, nonliteral language. When we say that "work was a living hell," we don't really mean to say that we spent the day shoveling fire and ashes, but rather want to communicate, in no uncertain terms, that it was a hard day at the office. Used this way, a metaphor is a concise, memorable, and often colorful way to express emotions. In a deeper sense, metaphors represent not only language but also thought and action. Writing in *Metaphors We Live By*, the linguists George Lakoff and Mark Johnson suggest that "our ordinary conceptual system, in terms of which we think and act, is fundamentally metaphorical in nature."[4]

But, Holland argues, metaphors are much more than merely a colorful form of speech, even more than representations of thoughts. They can also help us translate ideas into models. And that, he says, represents the basis of innovative thinking. In the same way that a metaphor helps communicate one concept by comparing it to another concept that is widely understood, using a simple model to describe one idea can help us grasp the complexities of a similar idea. In both cases we are using one concept (the *source*) to better understand another (the *target*). In this way, metaphors not only express existing ideas, they stimulate new ones.

In the book *Connections*, based on a memorable PBS series, James Burke describes several cases in which inventors were led to a discovery by first observing the similarities that existed between a previous invention (source) and that which the inventor wished to build (target). The automobile is a prime example. The carburetor is linked to a perfume sprayer, which in turn is linked to an eighteenth-century Italian who was trying to understand how to harness the hydraulic power of water. Allesandro Volta's electric pistol, initially created to test the purity of air, eventually sparked the fuel sprayed by the carburetor 125 years later. An automobile's gears are the direct descendants of the waterwheel, and the engine's pistons and cylinders can be traced to Thomas Newcomen's pumping engine, originally designed to drain coal mines. Each major discovery is connected to an earlier idea, a model that stimulated original thinking.

In our case, the main subject we wish to understand better (the target model) is the stock market or the economy. Over the years we have accumulated countless source models within the finance discipline to explain these phenomena, but too often they fail us. In many ways, the operation of markets and economies is still a mystery. Perhaps it is time we expanded the number of disciplines we call upon in our search for understanding. The more disciplines we have to explore, the more likely are we to find commonalities of mechanisms that clarify the mysteries. Innovative thinking, which is our goal, most often occurs when two or more mental models act in combination.

•   ■   •

LATTICEWORK IS ITSELF A METAPHOR. And on the surface, quite a simple one at that. Everyone knows what lattice-work is, and most people have some degree of firsthand experience with it. There is probably not a do-it-yourselfer in America who hasn't made good use of a four-by-eight sheet of latticework at some point. We use it to decorate fences, to create shade over patios, and to support climbing plants. It is but a very small stretch to envision a metaphorical lattice as the support structure for organizing a set of mental concepts.

Yet like many ideas that at first seem simple, the more closely we examine the metaphor of latticework, the more complex it becomes, and the more difficult to retain as a pure mental concept. One thing we understand about the human mind is the variability with which it receives and processes information. Any educator knows that the best way to teach a new idea to one student will have no effect whatsoever with another; the best educators, therefore, carry with them a virtual key ring with many different keys for unlocking individual minds.

In much the same way, I have found myself using various analogies to present the concept of a latticework of mental models. For those with a high-technology background, I often compare the process of constructing a mental latticework to designing a neural network, and they instantly recognize the possibilities for immense power. Talking with mathematicians, I may ask them to think about the concepts first envisioned by George

Boole and later formalized by Garrett Birkhoff of Harvard University in his book entitled *Lattice Theory*; this gives us the double reinforcement of a comparable theoretical framework that happens to be called by the very same name. Psychologists easily relate latticework to connectionism; educators link it with the brain's capacity to seek and find patterns. For people whose intellectual comfort zone is firmly planted in the humanities, I talk about the value of metaphors as devices for expanding the scope of our understanding. Many others, nonscientists like myself, often respond best to my description of a real piece of latticework with tiny lights at the junction points.

I hit upon this analogy one afternoon while staring out the window at the fence in our backyard. The entire fence is topped with a strip of decorative latticework that is visually broken into sections that echo the sections of the fence itself, as defined by the posts. Looking at this fence, thinking about mental models, I gradually began to see each section of latticework as one area of knowledge; the section nearest the garage became psychology, the next one biology, and so on. Within each section, it was easy to think of the points where two lattice strips connect as nodes. Then, in that way the brain skips from one analogy to the next, I suddenly thought of outdoor Christmas decorations and I began to see, in my mind's eye, miniature lightbulbs at each node.

Suppose I were struggling to understand some marketplace trend or make an investment decision, and I arrayed my uncertainty on that latticework. Looking at the question from the perspective of biology, I might see several lights pop on. When I moved to the next section, perhaps psychology, maybe a few other bulbs would light up. If I also got lights in a third section, and then a fourth, I would know I could proceed with reasonable confidence, for my original insecure thinking would now have been confirmed and ratified. Conversely, if I saw no lights going on while I pondered the problem, I would take that as a clear indication not to proceed.

That's the power of a latticework of mental models, and it extends far beyond the narrow question of picking stocks. It leads to understanding the full range of market forces—new businesses and trends, emerging markets, the flow of money, international shifts, the economy in general, and the actions of people in markets.

● ■ ●

TWO YEARS AFTER Charlie Munger startled the finance students at USC by challenging them to consider investing as a subdivision of worldly wisdom, he reprised his notion of a latticework of models at Stanford Law School, this time in somewhat more detail.[5]

He first reiterated his basic theme: true and lasting success comes to those who make the effort to first build a latticework of mental models, and then learn to think in an associative, multidisciplinary manner. It may take some work, he warned, especially if your education has forced you to specialize. But once those models are firmly set in your mind, you are intellectually equipped to deal with many different kinds of situations. "You can reach out and grasp the model that better solves the overall problem. All you have to do is know it and develop the right mental habits." No doubt Benjamin Franklin would approve.

I believe extraordinary rewards are in prospect to those who are willing to undertake the discovery of combinations between mental models. When that happens, then what Charlie calls "especially big forces" take over. This is more than one plus one plus one; it's the explosive power of critical mass, what Munger—the master of colorful language—calls "the lollapalooza effect."

This is the heart of the investing philosophy that is presented in this book: developing the ability to think of finance and investing as one piece of a unified whole, one segment of a body of knowledge. Done right, it produces nothing short of the lollapalooza effect. I believe it is our best hope for long-term investment success.

Let's give Charlie the final word on the subject. In response to questions from the Stanford students concerned about the process of uncovering the models, he remarked:

"Worldly wisdom is mostly very, very simple. There are a relatively small number of disciplines and a relatively small number of truly big ideas. And it's a lot of fun to figure it out. Even better, the fun never stops. Furthermore, there's a lot of money in it, as I can testify from my own personal experience.

"What I'm urging on you is not that hard to do. And the rewards are awesome.... It'll help you in business. It'll help you in law. It'll help you in life. And it'll help you in love.... It makes you better able to serve others, it makes you better able to serve yourself, and it makes life more fun."

CHAPTER 2

PHYSICS: THE POINT
OF EQUILIBRIUM

Physics is the science that investigates matter, energy, and the interaction between them—the study, in other words, of how our universe works. It encompasses all the forces that control motion, sound, light, heat, electricity, and magnetism, and their occurrence in all forms, from the smallest subatomic particles to entire solar systems. It is the intellectual foundation of many well-recognized principles such as gravitation and such mind-boggling modern concepts as quantum mechanics and relativity.

This is all very serious stuff, and frequently intimidating to nonscientists. Does it have a place in our latticework of mental models for investors? I believe it does.

Of course many people assume that physics is too hard for ordinary mortals to grasp or too abstract to have any real application to modern finance. If you are among them, think for a moment about the last time you visited an antiques store. If the shop owner has too much inventory, prices suddenly become negotiable; if you fall in love with a special one-of-a-kind item, you know that it will command a high price because it is rare but you may be willing to pay the price because your desire to own the item is equally high. What happens in that shop is governed by the rule of supply and demand, which in turn is a pure, classic example of the law of equilibrium at work. And equilibrium is one of the fundamental concepts in the field of physics.

How these concepts were uncovered, and the degree to which they may now be evolving into somewhat different forms, with profound implications for finance and economics, is the story of this chapter.

• ▪ •

THE HEART OF THE STORY begins with Sir Isaac Newton, the man whom many historians consider the greatest scientific mind of all time. He was born on Christmas Day in 1642, at the family farm in Lincolnshire, England. Nothing about the family circumstances at the time would have indicated that the premature, sickly infant would develop into a genius who would later be knighted Sir Isaac Newton. His father, who could neither read nor write, died several months before Isaac was born. Financially destitute, his mother was forced to leave the baby in the care of his grandmother for nine years. The youngster busied himself crafting intricately designed windmills, water clocks, and mouse-driven corn mills. It was a practice that served him well later, when he constructed his own scientific apparatuses to conduct experiments. Then, at age nineteen, with no formal background in mathematics or science, Newton stepped into Trinity College at Cambridge and into a dazzling world filled with new ideas.

In 1661, the year Newton began his studies at Cambridge, nearly everyone—academics and laypeople alike—believed that

God governed the world through inexplicable, supernatural powers. But the movement we now call the scientific revolution was already under way. Outside their formal classrooms, the students at Cambridge were exploring bold and contradictory ideas from the seventeenth century's greatest scientists: Johannes Kepler, Galileo Galilei, and René Descartes. Their ideas galvanized the students. What Newton learned from these three eventually led him to a new vision of the workings of the universe, and in particular the law of equilbrium.

JOHANNES KEPLER BEGAN his scientific career as an assistant to Tycho Brahe, a Danish nobleman and scientist, who had designed and built a large quadrant to study the movement of the planets. At that time, astronomers were pulled between two competing theories of the universe. One, originally suggested by Aristotle and amended by Ptolemy some four hundred years later, held that the sun, stars, and planets revolved around the earth. The other, published in 1543 by the Polish astronomer Nicolaus Copernicus and widely considered heretical well into the seventeenth century, held that the sun was at rest and all the planets, including the earth, were in motion around it.

Before Brahe, scientists in both camps had to depend on the naked eye for celestial measurements; the telescope had not yet been invented. Brahe's quadrant looked something like a gunsight and was able to record the positions of planets as two angles, one measured up from the horizon and the second measured around from true north.

Over a span of twenty-five years, Brahe recorded in meticulous detail the positions of planets. Just before his death in 1601, he turned over his observations to his young assistant. A talented mathematician, Kepler reanalyzed Brahe's detailed findings and began to draw meaningful conclusions that he summarized as the three major laws of planetary motion. By the time Newton was at Cambridge, Kepler's laws had begun to overrule the existing geocentric theories of astronomy and firmly established the sun as the center of the universe.

The lesson Newton took from Kepler is one that has been repeated many times throughout history: Our ability to answer even the most fundamental aspects of human existence depends largely upon the measuring instruments available at the time and the ability of scientists to apply rigorous mathematical reasoning to the data.

THE SECOND INFLUENCE on Newton's thinking was the work of Galileo Galilei, who died the year Newton was born. Galileo, the Italian philosopher, mathematician, inventor, and physicist, is considered to be the first modern-day experimental scientist. Among his many inventions are the thermometer, the pendulum clock, the proportional compass used by draftsmen, and—most important for our story—the telescope. Galileo was thus the first to actually observe the heavenly bodies described by all the earlier astronomers: Kepler, Copernicus, Ptolemy, and Aristotle. With the technology of the magnifiying optical instrument, Galileo could prove once and for all that the earth was not the center of the universe.

Galileo promoted a mathematical view of science. He believed that numerical relationships could be discovered throughout nature, but hastened to add that their existence was not contradictory to the teachings of the Church. It was important, he felt, to distinguish between "God's word" and "God's work."

According to Galileo, primacy was in God's work, and it was the goal of scientists to discover the relationships in nature on the basis of logic. Today he is best remembered among scientists for his experimental techniques.

THE THIRD IMPORTANT influence on Newton was René Descartes, the French mathematician and scientist who is often called the father of modern philosophy. He was one of the first to oppose the Aristotelian view of the world and instead embrace an empirical and mechanistic approach. Descartes died in 1650, eight years after Newton was born, and his ideas were gaining acceptance in certain circles by the time Newton entered Cambridge.

Descartes promoted a mechanical view of the world. He argued that the only way to understand how something works is to build a mechanical model of it, even if that model is constructed only in our imagination. According to Descartes, the human body, a falling rock, a growing tree, or a stormy night all suggested that mechanical laws were at work. This mechanical view provided a powerful research program for the seventeenth-century scientists. It suggested that no matter how complex or difficult the observation, it was possible to discover the underlying mechanical laws to explain the phenomena.

WHEN NEWTON FIRST attended Cambridge, he was unaware of the new discoveries and theories of these three scientists. But with relentless study and by applying his own intense powers of concentration, Newton quickly grasped their basic ideas. What he did with those ideas is the crux of our story.

While still a student, Newton began to synthesize Kepler's celestial laws of planetary motion with Galileo's terrestrial laws of falling bodies, all embraced within Descartes's cosmological view that the universe must operate by fixed mechanical laws. This gave Newton an outline to begin formulating the universal laws of physics.

Then, in 1665, Newton's life took an unexpected turn. As the plague descended on London, Cambridge was shut down and Newton was forced to retreat to his family's farm. There, in solitude and quiet, Newton's genius sprang forth. During what has been described as the *annus mirabilis* (the "wonder year"), Newton brought forth new ideas with breathtaking speed. His first major discovery was the invention of fluxions, or what we now call calculus. Next he developed the theory of optics. Previously it was believed that color was a mixture of light and darkness. But in a series of experiments using a prism in a darkened room, Newton discovered that light was made up of a combination of the colors of the spectrum. The highlight of that year, however, was Newton's discovery of the universal law of gravitation.

According to the legend, Newton watched an apple fall from a tree and, in a flash of insight, conceived of the idea of gravitation. Whereas Kepler had defined the three laws of planetary motion and Galileo had confirmed that a falling body accelerates at a uniform rate, Newton, in a stroke of genius, combined Kepler's laws with Galileo's observations. Newton reasoned that the force acting upon the apple was the same power holding the moon in orbit around the earth, and the planets around the sun. It was an incredible leap of intuition.

Surprisingly, Newton did not publish his discovery of gravitation for more than twenty years. Unable at first to present his findings with mathematical precision, he waited until the publication of his masterpiece, *Principia Mathematica,* to describe his three laws of motion.[1] Using these three laws, Newton was able to demonstrate how gravitational force acts between two bodies. He showed that the planets remain in a fixed orbit because the velocity of their forward motion is balanced by the force of gravity pulling them toward the sun. Thus the two equal forces create a state of equilibrium.

Equilibrium is defined as a state of balance between opposing forces, powers, or influences. An equilibrium model typically identifies a system that is at rest; this is called "static equilibrium." When competing forces are matched, a system reaches dynamic equilibrium. A scale that is equally weighted on both sides is an example of static equilibrium. Fill a bathtub full of water and then turn off the faucet and you will observe static equilibrium. But if you unplug the drain and then turn on the faucet so the level of the bathtub does not change, you are witnessing dynamic equilibrium. Another example is the human body. It remains in dynamic equilibrium so long as the heat loss from cooling remains in balance with the consumption of sugars.

With the publication of *Principia,* scientists quickly embraced the belief that all of the natural world was governed by universal laws, rather than by a godhead whose will no human could ever know. It is impossible to overstate the significance of this shift. It represents nothing less than a complete reversal of the very foundation on which human existence was thought to rest. It meant that scientists no longer had to rely on divine revelation for understanding. If they could discern the natural laws of the universe, they would be able to predict the future based on the present data. The scientific process used to investigate those natural laws is the legacy of Isaac Newton.

The Newtonian view of the world portrays science as the study of an ordered universe that is as predictable as a clock. Indeed, the metaphor frequently used for the Newtonian vision is a "clockwork universe." Just as we can understand how a clock functions by separating its mechanism into individual parts, we can understand the universe by analyzing its separate elements. At its core, this is the definition of physics: reducing phenomena into a few fundamental particles and defining the forces that act on those particles. For more than three hundred years, breaking apart nature into its constituent parts has become the primary activity of science.

PHYSICS HAS ALWAYS held an enviable position within the sciences. With its mathematical precision and immutable laws, it seduces us with a sense of certainty and gives us the comfort of absolute answers. We should not be surprised to learn, therefore, that other disciplines generally looked first to physics in a search for answers, for order underneath nature's messiness. In the nineteenth century, for instance, certain scholars wondered whether it was possible to apply the Newtonian vision to the affairs of man. Adolphe Quetelet, a Belgian mathematician known for applying probability theory to social phenomena, introduced the idea of "social physics." Auguste Comte, whom we shall meet again in Chapter 4, developed a science for explaining social organizations and guiding social planning, a science he called "sociology." Economists, too, have turned their attention to the Newtonian paradigm and the laws of physics.

After Newton, scholars in many fields focused their attention on systems that demonstrate equilibrium (whether static or dynamic), believing that it is nature's ultimate goal. If any deviations in the forces occurred, it was assumed that the deviations were small and temporary—the system would always revert back to equilibrium. The critical point for our story is how the concept of equilibrium expanded from celestial mechanics into much broader applications, particularly in economics.

• ■ •

FOR MORE THAN TWO HUNDRED YEARS, economists have relied on equilibrium theory to explain the behavior of economies. Alfred Marshall, the British economist, was the chief proponent of the concept of dynamic equilibrium in economics. His celebrated text, *Principles of Economics,* originally published in 1890, is considered one of the most important contributions to economic literature. In Book V of *Principles of Economics,* which addresses the relationship of demand, supply and price, Marshall devotes three separate chapters to economic equilibrium: in individuals, companies, and the marketplace.

In regard to individuals, Marshall eplains:

The simplest case of balance or equilibrium between desire and effort is found when a person satisfies one of his wants by his own direct work. When a boy picks blueberries for his own eating, the action of picking is probably itself pleasurable for a while; and for some time longer the pleasure of eating is more than enough to repay the trouble of picking. But after he has eaten a good deal, the desire for more diminishes; while the task of picking begins to cause weariness, which may indeed be a feeling of monotony rather than of fatigue. Equilibrium is reached when at last his eagerness to play and his disinclination for the work of picking counterbalance the desire for eating.[2]

In explaining how equilibrium affects companies, Marshall writes: "A Business firm grows and attains great strength, and afterwards perhaps stagnates and decays; and at the turning point there is a balancing or equilibrium of forces of life and decay."[3]

Even in the marketplace, the forces of equilibrium work to maintain a balance between demand and supply and help set prices for goods. According to Marshall: "When the demand price is equal to the supply price, the amount produced has no tendency either to be increased or to be diminished; it is in equilibrium."[4]

In Marshall's opinion, when the economy reaches equilibrium, it achieves stability. In fact, Marshall believed that equilibrium is the natural state of the economy; if the prices, demand, or supply become displaced, the economy will work to return to its natural equilibrium state. Here is his eloquent argument:

When demand and supply are in stable equilibrium, if any accident should move the scale of production from its equilibrium position, there will be instantly brought into play forces tending to push it back to that position; just as a stone hanging by a string is displaced from its equilibrium position, the force of gravity will at once tend to bring it back to its equilibrium position. The movements of the scale of production about its position of equilibrium will be of a somewhat similar kind.[5]

Marshall's *Principles of Economics* was the standard economics textbook for much of the twentieth century, until Paul Samuelson introduced his *Economics* in 1948. Although colleges soon favored Samuelson's updated text over Marshall's classic work, the message of equilibrium remained the same. According to Samuelson, millions of prices and millions of outputs are connected to an interdependent weblike system. Within this system, households with preferences for products and services interact with firms that provide those products and services. These firms, each guided by a desire to maximize profits, transform information from households into products sold to households. The logical structure of this exchange, says Samuelson, is a general equilibrium system.

Paul Samuelson, who won the Nobel Prize in economics in 1970, is a man of great intellect. The stock market fascinates him, and he takes a suspicious view of any professional who claims to be able to predict price changes and thus beat the market. "The respect for evidence," he once wrote, "compels me to incline toward the hypothesis that most portfolio decision makers should go out of business—take up plumbing, teach Greek, or help produce the annual GNP by serving as corporate executives."[6]

An important part of our story is tracing how Samuelson, with his respect for evidence and scientific methods, developed his own theories of how the market establishes prices. And, in yet another demonstration of the cumulative nature of human knowledge, we learn that Samuelson's attitude about the market was shaped by the work of Louis Bachelier, Maurice Kendall, and Alfred Cowles.

IN 1932, ALFRED COWLES established the Cowles Commission for Research and Economics. Having subscribed to several investment services, none of which predicted the 1929 stock market crash, Cowles set about to determine whether market forecasters could actually predict the future direction of the market. In one of the most detailed studies ever conducted, the commission analyzed 6,904 forecasts from 1929 through 1944; according to Cowles, "the results failed to disclose evidence of ability to predict successfully the future course of the stock market."[7]

Maurice Kendall, a professor of statistics at the London School of Economics, looked past the market forecasters the Cowles Commission studied and instead analyzed individual stock prices. In a 1953 paper entitled "The Analysis of Economic Time Series," Kendall studied the behavior of stock prices dating back over fifty years and was unable to find any pattern or structure in prices that would lead someone to make an accurate forecast. According to Peter Bernstein, whose *Capital Ideas* explores the origins of modern financial theory, Samuelson's interest in the stock market was triggered in large part by the news that Kendall's paper was greeted enthusiastically at the Royal Statistical Society.

In thinking about Kendall's work, Samuelson connected the idea of stock price movements with the classical economic theory of price and value. For nearly two hundred years, since the 1776 publication of Adam Smith's *The Wealth of Nations,* economists had agreed there is a fundamental value, the "true value," that underlies the marketplace, and that prices tend to bounce above and below this value. Of course, what has haunted economists and investors alike ever since is the debate over what is the true value. Alfred Marshall tells us competition ultimately determines equilibrium price. If price is oscillating, it is because there is a temporary imbalance between supply and demand, but this is ultimately corrected by the marketplace.

For his part, Samuelson believed stock prices bounced around because of the perceived uncertainty over a stock's future value. Whether IBM is worth $100 per share or $50 per share is a debate in the marketplace over the future growth of its earnings, the competitive landscape, and attitudes about inflation and interest rates. In his landmark 1965 paper, "Proof That Properly Anticipated Prices Fluctuate Randomly," Samuelson introduced the concept of "shadow prices"—a stock's intrinsic, but perhaps not obvious, value. Of course the problem is how to bring shadow prices to the forefront of the market. What Samuelson did next created a seismic shift in how some people began to frame the behavior of the stock market.

Relying on a little-known doctoral dissertation written in 1900 by the French mathematician Louis Bachelier, Samuelson began to weave together a theory of market prices. Bachelier had argued that price changes in the market were impossible to predict. His reasoning was straightforward. "Contradictory opinions concerning market changes diverge so much," he wrote, "that at the same instant buyers believe in a price increase and sellers believe in price decrease." Believing, on average, that neither buyers nor sellers possessed any greater insight, Bachelier made a startling conclusion. "It seems that the market, the aggregate of speculators, at a given instant can believe in neither a market rise nor a market fall, since, for each quoted price, there are as many buyers as sellers." Thus, according to Bachelier, "the mathematical expectation of the speculator is zero."[8]

Bachelier's logic gave Samuelson a pathway for moving his shadow prices from behind the market to the forefront. In one giant leap, Samuelson suggested that the best measure of shadow prices was Bachelier's market prices. It may not always be perfectly accurate, he said, but there was no better way to gauge intrinsic value than by Bachelier's aggregated collection of buyers and sellers.

To strengthen the shadow price theory, Samuelson next introduced the "rational expectations hypothesis." Samuelson writes, "We would expect people in the marketplace, in pursuit of avid and intelligent self-interest, to take account of those elements of future events that in a probability sense may be discerned to be casting their shadows before them."[9] Samuelson, in other words, believed that people make rational decisions consistent with their individual preferences. Hence, stock prices at any point in time are a reflection of these rational decisions; thus shadow prices and market prices become one and the same.

Another way to think about this is that Samuelson took the concept of equilibrium in the economy and moved it to the stock market, connecting the idea of stock price movement with the classical idea that price and value exist in equilibrium. His notion that investors act on the basis of rational expectations is what upholds the concept of equilibrium in the stock market.

●　■　●

THE INDIVIDUAL CREDITED WITH taking Samuelson's theoretical view of the market to the next level is Eugene Fama. His University of Chicago doctoral dissertation entitled "The Behavior of Stock Prices" immediately caught the attention of the investment community. The dissertation was published in its entirety in the *Journal of Business* in 1965 and was later excerpted in *The Financial Analysts Journal* and *Institutional Investor*. It is the foundation of what has come to be called "modern portfolio theory."

Fama's message was clear. Stock prices are not predictable because the market is too efficient. In an efficient market, a great many smart people (Fama called them "rational profit maximizers") have simultaneous access to all the relevant information, and they aggressively apply that information in a way that causes prices to adjust instantaneously—thus restoring equilibrium—before anyone can profit. Predictions about the future therefore have no place in an efficient market, because the share prices fully reflect all available information. It's important to remember that Fama's efficient market theory is applicable only in the much broader view of market equilibrium promoted by Marshall, Samuelson, and one other economist: William Sharpe.

Sharpe was awarded the 1990 Nobel Prize in economics for developing "a market equilibrium theory of asset prices under conditions of risk." His theory was originally outlined in a 1964 paper entitled "Capital Asset Prices: A Theory of Market Equilibrium under Conditions of Risk." Sharpe explained, "In equilibrium, there is a simple linear relationship between the expected return and standard deviation of return (defined as risk)."[10] According to Sharpe, the only way to achieve a greater return is to incur additional risk. To increase expected returns, investors need only march further out on the capital market line. Conversely, if investors wished to assume less risk, they would step down the capital line and by doing so receive less return. In either case, equilibrium is maintained.

•   ■   •

THE CONCEPT OF EQUILIBRIUM is so deeply embedded in our theory of economics and the stock market, it is difficult to imagine any other idea of how these systems could possibly work. As we have seen, equilibrium is not only the backbone for classical economics but it also serves as the foundation for modern portfolio theory. To question the validity of the equilibrium model is to enter into combat with a legion of scholars who have made it their career to defend this ideal. Although the analogy may be a stretch, debating existing economic dogma is not unlike the challenge Copernicus faced when he questioned the religious view of a geocentric universe. Yet despite the risk, a number of scientists have begun to question the equilibrium theory that dominates our view of the economy and the stock market.

ONE PLACE WHERE THE QUESTION is being raised is the Santa Fe Institute, where scientists from several disciplines are studying complex adaptive systems—those systems with many interacting parts that are continually changing their behavior in response to changes in the environment. A simple system, in contrast, has very few interacting parts. Examples of complex adaptive systems include central nervous systems, ecologies, ant colonies, political systems, social structures, and economies. To this list of complex adaptive systems we must add one more: stock markets.

Every complex adaptive system is actually a network of many individual agents all acting in parallel and interacting with one another. The critical variable that makes a system both complex and adaptive is the idea that agents (neurons, ants, or investors) in the system accumulate experience by interacting with other agents and then change themselves to adapt to a changing environment. No thoughtful person, looking at the present stock market, can fail to conclude that it shows all the traits of a complex adaptive system. And this takes us to the crux of the matter: If a complex adaptive system is, by definition, *continuously adapting*, it is impossible for any such system, including the stock market, ever to reach a state of perfect equilibrium.

What does that mean for the market? It throws the classic theories of economic equilibrium into serious question.[11] The standard equilibrium theory is rational, mechanistic, and efficient. It assumes that identical individual investors share rational expectations about stock prices and then efficiently discount that information into the market. It further assumes there are no profitable strategies available that are not already priced into the market.

The counterview from Santa Fe suggests the opposite: A market that is not rational, is organic rather than mechanistic, and is imperfectly efficient. It assumes the individual agents are in fact irrational and hence will misprice securities, creating the possibility for profitable strategies. (In later chapters we will consider the underlying psychology that causes people to behave irrationally where money is concerned.)

The catalyst for this alternative view of markets was the 1987 stock market crash. According to classical market theory, sudden price changes occur because rational investors adjust to new market information. However, several post-1987 studies failed to identify any information that might have caused a correlating decline in price. In a strict interpretation of market equilibrium, there would be no booms or crashes, no high trading volume or high turnover ratios. But as we know all too well, trading volume and turnover ratios have continued to climb, and heightened volatility has become the norm rather than the exception. Is it possible that automatic acceptance of market equilibrium, and the efficient market hypothesis that is its corollary, can no longer be defended?

In all fairness, I must point out that classical economists and proponents of modern portfolio theory recognize that their systems are not capable of perfect equilibrium. Near the end of his life, even Alfred Marshall was not entirely convinced (see footnote 5 in Chapter 3). Paul Samuelson acknowledges that people do not begin with perfect rationality but believes that over time the rational and thoughtful investor will win out over the irrational and the visceral. Likewise, Fama believes that an efficient market requires neither total rationality nor perfect information; however, because it *is* efficient, he says, it is all but impossible for any one individual to beat the market.

HOW, THEN, DOES THE efficient market hypothesis account for the incredible investment results of Benjamin Graham, Warren Buffett, Peter Lynch, and Bill Miller, or explain the various strategies that have managed to beat the market in the recent past? Andrew Lo, professor of finance at the Massachusetts Institute of Technology and coauthor of *A Non-Random Walk down Wall Street,* points out that "over the past three decades, a number of studies have reported so-called anomalies, strategies that, when applied to historical data, lead to return differences that are not easily explained by risk differences."[12] These anomalies include "size effects" (the idea that excess returns accrue to small-capitalization stocks), "calendar effects" (the idea that small-capitalization stocks outperform large-capitalization stocks by a large margin at the turn of the calendar year), and the "*Value Line* enigma" (a study that proved *Value Line*'s top-rated stocks have consistently beaten the market over time).

We are forced to conclude that the efficient market hypothesis has its flaws. Because of the anomalies mentioned just above and, more important, because of factors of psychology and human nature we shall consider in later chapters, we cannot say that all prices for all stocks will always accurately reflect the state of affairs. Andrew Lo, in fact, maintains that there is no consensus among financial experts about the efficient market hypothesis, and I believe that he is correct. For my part, I suspect that most economists, if pressed, would confess that the idea of a market composed of only rational investors who process perfect information is an idealized system, displaying all the limitations inherent in any idealized system. Louis Bachelier's equal number of buyers and sellers who exhibit Samuelson's rationality and process Fama's perfect information is obviously at odds with what occurs in the real world of investing. Investment professionals who continue to promote an idealized system over what is exhibited in the real system may be leading us down the wrong path.

Yet we still hold on to our belief that the law of equilibrium is absolute and rules finance, economies, and markets unequivocally. We cling to it because the entire Newtonian system, of which equilibrium is one part, has been our model for how to think about the world for three hundred years. Letting go of such deeply embedded ideas is not easy. However, in the spirit of Newton, and Galileo, and Copernicus, we must be willing to see the world as it is, and that means making room for new ideas.

Let me say very clearly here that I am not asking you to surrender your trust in equilibrium, or to conclude that the law of supply and demand is hereby revoked. The world is not nearly so simple that I could make such black-and-white dictums—and that, in fact, is the point. In an environment of complexity, simple laws are insufficient to explain the entire system.

Equilibrium may indeed be the natural state of the world, and restoring it when it is disturbed may be nature's goal, but it is not the constant condition that Newtonian physics would suggest. At any given moment, *both* equilibrium and disequilibrium may be found in the market. It's a bit like those trick photographs that show two different scenes; one well-known example seems at first to depict a wineglass, until you shift your perspective and see that it also portrays a silhouette of a woman in an old-fashioned dress. Both images are correct, both exist simultaneously. Which one we focus on is a matter of personal perspective. In much the same way, the balance between supply and demand, between price and value, will always be in evidence in the daily operation of the market, but it no longer gives us the full answer.

Just as our viewpoint of the world changed when it was demonstrated the earth was no longer the center of the universe, so will our viewpoint of the market change, I believe, when we accept that it is not governed strictly by the mechanical laws of Newton, but that other forces are also at work.

The obvious question then becomes, if the Newtonian perspective is inadequate by itself, what else should we add? The answer, described in the following chapter, may surprise you.

CHAPTER 3

BIOLOGY: THE ORIGIN OF A NEW SPECIES

The market crash of 1987 caught most economists, scholars, and investment professionals by surprise. Nowhere in the classical, equilibrium-based view of the market so long considered inviolate was there anything that would predict or even describe the events of 1987. This failure of the existing theory left open the potential for competing theories. Chief among them is the belief that the market and the economy are best understood from a *biological* perspective.

Turning to biology for insight into finance and investing may at first seem a startling move, but just as we did in our study of physics, we focus here on just one core idea from the field of biology: evolution. Whereas in nature the process of evolution is one of natural selection, seeing the market within an evolutionary framework allows us to observe the law of economic selection.

The concept of evolution is not the sole intellectual franchise of any one mind. As far back as the sixth century B.C., the possibility of species developing in different forms had been expressed by Greek and Chinese philosophers. Yet today the evolutionary principle is firmly associated with one individual, a man whose ideas triggered a scientific revolution every bit as profound as that emanating from the work of Isaac Newton a century and a half earlier.

•　■　•

CHARLES ROBERT DARWIN was born in Shrewsbury, England, in 1809, into a family of scientists. His paternal grandfather was the physician and scientist Erasmus Darwin, and on his mother's side, his grandfather was the famous potter Josiah Wedgwood.[1] His father, also a respected physician and a very forceful personality, insisted that Charles study medicine, and enrolled him at the University of Edinburgh. Darwin was uninterested. He found the classroom studies boring and became violently ill at the sight of surgery performed without anesthesia. The natural world was far more fascinating to him, and Darwin spent many hours reading geology and collecting insects and other specimens.

Realizing his son would never become a physician, Robert Darwin sent Charles to Cambridge University to study divinity. Once again a less than stellar student, he nonetheless earned a bachelor's degree in theology. More significant than the formal course of study were the associations he formed with several of the Cambridge faculty. The Reverend John Stevens Henslow, professor of botany, permitted the enthusiastic amateur to sit in on his lectures and to accompany him on his daily walks to study plant life. Darwin spent so many hours in the professor's company that he was known around the university as "the man who walks with Henslow." After graduation, Darwin joined a geological field trip to Wales, an experience that moved him to consider a career as a geologist. But when he returned home from Wales, Darwin found waiting for him a letter that would change his life forever.

Professor Henslow wrote to say that he had recommended Darwin for the position of naturalist on a naval expedition. HMS *Beagle*, under the command of Captain Robert FitzRoy, was soon to leave on a voyage of scientific exploration with two purposes: to continue the process of charting the coast of South America, and to add to the investigation of longitude by taking a series of chronological readings. It would require sailing completely around the world, a trip of at least two years (as it turned out, the trip took five years). The position of naturalist carried no salary—in fact, the naturalist would have to pay his own expenses—but Darwin was thrilled at the prospect.

He almost did not make the journey. Faced with his father's strong objections, Charles at first declined the offer. Fortunately, Charles's uncle, Josiah Wedgwood II, whom Dr. Darwin respected, intervened and convinced his brother-in-law that it was a splendid opportunity for the young man. And thus when the *Beagle* set sail from Plymouth, England, on December 27, 1831, Charles Darwin was aboard, charged with the responsibility of collecting, recording, and analyzing all the flora and fauna, and every other aspect of the natural history, that would be encountered. He was twenty-two years old.

Always more comfortable on land than sea, Darwin was frequently seasick, and during the voyage he often kept to himself, reading from the ship's library and his own personal collection of scientific texts. But whenever the ship landed, he plunged eagerly into exploring the local environment. What we now know to be his most significant observations occurred fairly early in the trip, on the Galapagos Islands, near the equator on the Pacific side of South America, about 600 miles west of Ecuador. This island group would prove to be the perfect laboratory for studying the mutability of species.

Darwin the amateur geologist knew that the Galapagos were classed as oceanic islands, meaning they had risen from the sea by volcanic action with no life forms aboard. Nature creates these islands and then waits to see who shows up. An oceanic island eventually becomes inhabited but only by forms that can reach it by wing (birds) or by wind (spores and seeds). In the Galapagos, Darwin surmised that the tortoise and marine iguana, swimmers capable of staying under the water for long periods of time, could have made the long journey from South America, possibly attached to floating debris pulled along by the current. He also figured that other animals he observed had been brought to the islands by earlier sailors and adventurers. But much of what he saw in the island group puzzled and intrigued him.

Darwin was particularly fascinated by the presence of thirteen types of finches. He first assumed these Galapagos finches, today called Darwin's finches, were a subspecies of the South American finches he had studied earlier and had most likely been blown to sea in a storm. But as he studied distribution patterns, Darwin observed that most islands in the archipelago carried only two or three types of finches; only the larger central islands showed greater diversification. What intrigued him even more was that all the Galapagos finches differed in size and behavior. Some were heavy-billed seedeaters; others were slender billed and favored insects. Sailing through the archipelago, Darwin discovered that the finches on Hood Island were different from those on Tower Island and that both were different from those on Indefatigable Island. He began to wonder what would happen if a few finches on Hood Island were blown by high wind to another island. Darwin concluded that if the newcomers were pre-adapted to the new habitat, they would survive and multiply alongside the resident finches; if not, their numbers would quickly diminish. It was one thread of what would ultimately become his famous thesis.

When Darwin returned home in 1836, he was enthusiastically welcomed into England's scientific community. He was immediately made a fellow of the Geological Society and three years later was elected to the Royal Society. He quickly settled into work. Publicly, Darwin was busily preparing the publication of his many geological and biological discoveries. But privately, Darwin was also constructing a new theory.

Reviewing his notes from the voyage, Darwin was deeply perplexed. Why did the birds and tortoises on some islands in the Galapagos resemble the species found in South America while those on other islands did not? This observation was even more disturbing when Darwin learned that the finches he brought back from the Galapagos belonged to different species and were not simply different varieties of the same species, as he had previously believed. Darwin also discovered the mockingbirds he had collected were three distinct species and the tortoises represented two species. He began referring to these troubling questions as "the species problem," and outlined his observations in a notebook he later entitled "Notebook on the Transmutation of the Species."

Darwin now began an intense investigation into species variation. He devoured all the written work on the subject and exchanged voluminous correspondence with botanists, naturalists, and zookeepers—anyone who had information or opinions about species mutation. What he learned convinced him that he was on the right track with his working hypothesis: that species do in fact change, whether from place to place or from time period to time period. The idea was not only radical, it was blasphemous. Darwin struggled to keep his work secret.

As he continued to study and think, Darwin was increasingly certain that evolution was taking place, but he did not yet understand how. It wasn't until 1838 that he was able to put the pieces together. In the fall of that year, Darwin began to read *Essay on the Principle of Population* by the British economist Thomas Malthus. After exploring the relationship between the food supply and human population, Malthus concluded that population was increasing geometrically while the means of subsistence (food production) progressed arithmetically. Thus population growth would always outrun the growth of food supplies and populations would grow until checked by war, famine, or disease.

Darwin saw an immediate parallel between Malthus's work and the unanswered questions about animal and plant populations. Malthus's theory decreed that a limited food supply would force an increasing population into a permanent struggle for survival. From his years of observation, Darwin recognized the Malthusian process in the animal world. "Being well prepared to appreciate the struggle for existence which everywhere goes on from long-continued observation of the habits of animals and plants," he wrote in his notebook, "it at once struck me that under these circumstances, favorable variations would tend to be preserved and unfavorable ones to be destroyed. The result of this would be the formation of new species. Here, then, I had at last got a theory—a process by which to work."[2]

The originality of Darwin's theory lay in the idea that the struggle for survival was occurring not only between species but between individuals within the same species. If having a longer beak, for example, increased a bird's chances of survival, then more birds with long beaks would survive and would produce more offspring and thus would be more likely to pass this advantage on. Eventually, the longer beak would become dominant within the species.[3] By this process of natural selection, Darwin theorized, favorable variations are preserved and transmitted to succeeding generations. After several generations, small gradual changes in the species begin to add up to larger changes—thus evolution occurs.

By 1842, Darwin had completed a brief outline of his new theory, but he resisted publication. Perhaps sensing the furious controversy the theory would generate, he insisted on developing further documentation. Then on June 18, 1858, Darwin received a paper from the naturalist Alfred Russel Wallace that summarized perfectly the theory Darwin had been working on for twenty years. Darwin called upon two close colleagues, the geologist Robert Lyell and the botanist Joseph Hooker, for advice, and they decided to present the work of both men in a combined paper. The following year, Darwin published *On the Origin of Species by Means of Natural Selection, or the Preservation of Favoured Races in the Struggle for Life.* The book sold out on the first day, and by 1872, *The Origin of Species,* as it was popularly called, was in its sixth edition.

Darwin had written the book of the century—perhaps, said the noted evolutionary biologist Richard Dawkins, the book of the millennium. *"The Origin* changed humanity's view of humanity, and of all life, forever," Dawkins wrote.[4] It also changed our view of other areas of knowledge, including economics, and that is our focus in this chapter.

• ■ •

BRIAN ARTHUR, FORMERLY AT STANFORD University and now Citibank Professor of Economics at the Santa Fe Institute, was one of the first economists willing to take a fresh look at how economics really works. Trained in classical economics, Arthur was immersed in the teachings of Marshall and Samuelson and in particular the equilibrium of markets—the stability between supply and demand.[5] But the world described by the classical economists was not the same world Arthur saw. No matter how hard he tried to embrace the teachings of stability, he could see only instability. The world was constantly changing, thought Arthur. It was full of upheavals and surprises. It was continually evolving.

In November 1979, Arthur began to record his observations in his personal notebook. One page, which he entitled "Economics Old and New," he divided into two columns, in which he began to list the characteristics of both concepts. Under "Old Economics," Arthur listed investors as identical, rational, and equal in ability. The system was devoid of any real dynamics. Everything was in equilibrium. Economics was based on classical physics under the belief that the system was structurally simple. Under "New Economics," Arthur wrote that people were separate and different in ability. They were emotional. The system was complicated and ever-changing. In Arthur's mind, economics was not simple, but inherently complex, more akin to biology than physics.

A soft-spoken Irishman, Arthur confesses he was not the first to think about economics in this way, but he was most assuredly the first to confront it.

It was the Nobel Prize–winning economist Ken Arrow who first introduced Brian Arthur to the close-knit group of scientists working at the Santa Fe Institute. Arrow invited Arthur to attend a conference of physicists, biologists, and economists at the institute in the fall of 1987 to present his latest research. The conference was organized in the hope that the ideas percolating within natural sciences, namely "the science of complexity," would help stimulate new ways to think about economics.[6] Common to the study of complexity is the notion that complex adaptive systems operate with multiple elements, each adapting or reacting to the patterns the system itself creates. Complex adaptive systems are in a constant process of evolving over time. These types of systems are familiar to biologists and ecologists, but the group at Santa Fe thought that perhaps the concept should be expanded, that maybe now the time had come to include the study of economic systems and stock markets within the overarching idea of complexity.

Unshackling themselves from the classical teachings, the Santa Fe group was able to point out four distinct features they observed about the economy.

1. *Dispersed interaction:* What happens in the economy is determined by the interactions of a great number of individual agents all acting in parallel. The action of any one individual agent depends on the anticipated actions of a

limited number of agents as well as on the system they co-create.

2. *No global controller:* Although there are laws and institutions, there is no one global entity that controls the economy. Rather the system is controlled by the competition and coordination between the agents of the system.

3. *Continual adaptation:* The behavior, actions, and strategies of the agents, as well as their products and services, are revised continually on the basis of accumulated experience. In other words, the system adapts. It creates new products, new markets, new institutions, and new behaviors. It is an ongoing system.

4. *Out-of-equilibrium dynamics:* Unlike the equilibrium models that dominate the thinking in classical economics, the Santa Fe group believed the economy, because of its constant change, operates far from equilibrium.

An essential element of a complex adaptive system is a feedback loop. That is, agents in the system first form expectations, or models, and then act on the basis of predictions generated by these models. But over time these models change, depending on how accurately they predict the environment. If the model is useful, it is retained; if not, the agents alter the model to increase its predictability. Obviously, accuracy of predictability is a paramount concern to participants in the stock market, and we may be able to achieve broader understanding if we can learn to view the market as one type of complex adaptive system.

The whole notion of complex systems is a new way of seeing the world, and it is not easily grasped. How exactly do agents in a complex adaptive system interact? How do they go about collectively creating, and then changing, a model for predicting the future? For those of us who are not scientists, finding a way to visualize the process is helpful. Brian Arthur gives us an answer, with an example he has dubbed "the El Farol Problem."

El Farol, a bar in Santa Fe, New Mexico, used to feature Irish music on Thursday nights. Arthur, the Irishman, loved to go there to listen to his favorite music. On most occasions, the bar patrons were well behaved and it was enjoyable to sit and listen to the music. But on some nights, the bar was packed with so many people crammed together drinking and singing that the scene became unruly. Now Arthur was confronted with a problem: How could he decide which nights to go to El Farol and which nights to stay home? The chore of having to decide led him to formulate a mathematical theory he named the El Farol Problem. It has, he says, all the characteristics of a complex adaptive system.

Suppose, says Arthur, there are one hundred people in Santa Fe who are interested in going to El Farol to listen to Irish music, but none of the one hundred people wants to go if the bar is going to be crowded. Now also suppose the bar publishes its weekly attendance for the past ten weeks. With this information, the music lovers will build models to predict how many people will show up next Thursday. Some may figure that it will be approximately the same number of people from last week. Others will take an average of the last few weeks. A few will attempt to correlate attendance data to the weather or to other activities competing for the same audience. There are endless ways to build models to predict how many people will go to the bar.

Now let's say that every lover of Irish music decides that the comfort level in the small bar is sixty people. All one hundred people will decide, using whatever predictor has been the most accurate over the last few weeks, when that limit is going to be reached. Because each person has a different predictor, on any given Thursday some people will turn up at El Farol and others will stay home because their model has predicted more than sixty people will be attending. The following day, El Farol publishes its attendance and the hundred music lovers will update their models and get ready for next week's prediction.

The El Farol process can be termed an ecology of predictors, says Arthur. At any point, there is a group of models that are deemed "alive"—that is, they are useful predictors of how many people will attend the bar. Conversely, predictors that turn out to be inaccurate will slowly die off. Each week, new predictors, new models, new beliefs will compete for use by other music lovers.

We can quickly see how the El Farol process echoes the Darwinian idea of survival through natural selection, and how logically this extends to economies and markets. In the markets, each agent's predictive models compete for survival against the models of all other agents, and the feedback that is generated causes some models to be changed and others to disappear. It is a world, says Arthur, that is complex, adaptive, and evolutionary.

Right about now you may be wondering the same things I wondered when I first heard about the El Farol Problem. Is it anything more than a mildly entertaining theory formulated to help us understand the challenges of predicting complex adaptive systems? Does it actually exist in the market? The answer to both questions is yes.

●　■　●

EACH YEAR MERRILL LYNCH POLLS a group of institutional investors about the factors that most influence their stock selection. Participants are asked to rank twenty-three different factors:

1. earnings per share surprise
2. return on equity
3. earnings revisions
4. price to cash flow
5. projected five-year profit growth
6. debt to equity
7. earnings per share momentum
8. relative strength
9. price to earnings
10. price to book
11. analysts' opinion changes
12. earnings variability
13. dividend discount model
14. price to sales
15. neglected stocks
16. beta
17. earnings estimate dispersion
18. dividend yield
19. earnings uncertainty
20. foreign exposure
21. size
22. low stock price
23. interest rate sensitivity

All these factors represent belief models that investors use to predict the behavior of stock prices. Comparing polls from several years, we can see how the models change in popularity over time.

In the late 1980s and early 1990s, the most popular choices were debt to equity, earnings yields, and price to book. Leveraged buyouts were commonplace then, and these models were helpful for identifying potential takeouts. But as these models became less effective at predicting stock price appreciation, they were soon underemphasized. In recent years, the most popular factors have been earnings surprise, price to cash flow, and return on equity.

I believe the Merrill Lynch survey is an excellent example of Arthur's El Farol Problem applied to the investment world. We can say all of these twenty-three models form an ecology of co-evolving hypotheses. As the environment changes, some models die away and others come to life. This is the essence of evolution—what we might call applied evolution—as it plays out in the field of economics.

●　■　●

BRIAN ARTHUR is not the only Santa Fe scientist exploring the link between biology and economics. Doyne Farmer, originally trained as a physicist, knew that classical economics was based on the same equilibrium laws he had studied in college, but he also knew that what he observed in the markets did not always correspond with those laws.

Farmer was already convinced that the market was not efficient. That much was clear to him. Lawrence Summers, who was to become U.S. Treasury Secretary, was one of the original attendees at the 1987 Santa Fe conference on economics and complex systems. Summers researched the one hundred largest daily market moves and was able to connect newsworthy events to only 40 percent of them. In other words, more than half of the largest market moves were occurring without some corresponding informational input. This, Farmer knew, was highly inconsistent with the efficient market theory. It was clear that some internal dynamics were causing the excess volatility in the market. But what were those dynamics? Farmer, who possesses a natural sense of curiosity that constantly pushes him into new arenas, thought that the answer might be found, not in the laws that explain celestial mechanics, but rather in the laws that describe the behavior of ecological systems.

In a Santa Fe Institute working paper titled "Market Force, Ecology, and Evolution," Farmer has taken the important first step in outlining the behavior of the stock market in biological terms. His analogy between a biological ecology of interacting species and a financial ecology of interacting strategies is summarized in the table shown here.[7]

BIOLOGICAL ECOLOGY	FINANCIAL ECOLOGY
Species	Trading strategy
Individual organism	Trader
Genotype (genetic constitution)	Functional representation of strategy
Phenotype (observable appearance)	Actions of the strategy (buying and selling)
Population	Capital
External environment	Price and other informational inputs
Selection	Capital allocation
Mutation and recombination	Creation of new strategies

Farmer is the first to confess the analogy is not perfect, but it does present a stimulating way in which to think about the market. Furthermore it links the process to a clearly defined science of how living systems behave and evolve.

If we go back through the history of the stock market and seek to identify the major trading strategies that dominated the landscape, I propose there have been four major strategies (which in Farmer's analogy would be species). In the 1930s and 1940s, the discount-to-hard-book-value strategy, first proposed by Benjamin Graham and David Dodd in their classic 1934 textbook *Security Analysis,* was dominant. After World War II and into the 1950s, the second major strategy that dominated finance was the dividend model. As the memories of the 1929 market crash faded and prosperity unfolded after World War II, investors were increasingly attracted to stocks that paid high dividends, and lower-paying bonds lost favor. By the 1960s, a third strategy appeared. Investors exchanged stocks paying high dividends for companies that were expected to grow earnings. By the 1980s a fourth strategy took over. Investors began to favor cash-flow models over the earnings model. Today, although it is not perfectly clear, it appears that a fifth strategy is emerging: cash return on invested capital.

Most of us easily recognize these well-known strategies, and we can readily accept the idea that each one gained favor by overtaking a previously dominant strategy and was then itself eventually overtaken by a new strategy. In a word, evolution took place in the stock market via economic selection.

How does economic selection occur? Remember that in Doyne Farmer's analogy, a biological population is capital and natural selection occurs by allocation of capital. This means that capital varies in relation to the popularity of a strategy. If a strategy is successful, it attracts more capital and becomes the dominant strategy. When a new strategy is discovered, capital is re–allocated—or, in biological terms, there is a change in population. As Farmer notes, "The long-term evolution of the market can be studied in terms of flows of money. Financial evolution is influenced by money in much the same way that biological evolution is influenced by food."[8]

Why are financial strategies so diverse? The answer, Farmer believes, starts with the idea that basic strategies induce patterns of behavior. Agents rush in to exploit these obvious patterns, causing an ultimate side effect. As more agents begin using the same strategy, its profitability drops. The inefficiency becomes apparent, and the original strategy is washed out. But then new agents enter the picture with new ideas. They form new strategies of which any number may become profitable. Capital shifts and the new strategy explodes, which starts the evolutionary process again.

Will the market ever become efficient? Likely not. Each strategy that eliminates an inefficiency will soon be replaced in turn by a new strategy. The market will always maintain some level of diversity, and this we know is a principal cause of evolution.

What we are learning is that studying economic and financial systems is very similar to studying biological systems. The central concept for both is the notion of change, what biologists call evolution. The models we use to explain the evolution of financial strategies are mathematically similar to the equations biologists use to study populations of predator-prey systems, competing systems, or symbiotic systems.

●　■　●

THE CONCEPT OF EVOLUTION should not be foreign to financial analysts. Outside the markets, we can easily observe the multitudes of systems that undergo change, from fashions to language to popular culture in all its manifestations. If understanding financial markets in terms of evolution seems intimidating to some, I suspect that may be because of the words that biologists use to describe the process: Variation. Adaptation. Mutation. Genetic recombination.

Perhaps it is easier if we switch to the vocabulary of the corporate world, where the concepts of managing change, encouraging innovation, and adapting to marketplace demands are well established and well understood. Simply put, the whole concept of adaptation is based on the idea that there is a problem and the species—or the industry, or the company—eventually solves it by adapting to the environment.

Now if we turn our attention to the financial markets, what do we see? The same phenomena of adaptation and change, merely in a different form. The Standard & Poor's 500-stock index of the 1960s hardly resembles today's index. In the 1960s the index was dominated by industrial and capital goods companies; in the year 2000 it was dominated by technology and finance companies. As we have already seen, investment strategies have changed as well. If you are still picking stocks using a discount-to-hard-book-value model or relying on dividend models to tell you when the stock market is over- or undervalued, it is unlikely you have enjoyed even average investment returns. If these models were the basic strategy for an investment firm in recent years, the firm probably either changed its models or went out of business. The common trait found in financial systems, just as in biological systems, is evolution—adaptation.

MANY FORWARD-THINKING PEOPLE, including several we have met in this chapter, believe that the theory of evolution may become the most powerful force in finance. "There are many opportunities for biological principles to be applied to financial interactions," Doyne Farmer explains; "after all, financial institutions are uniquely human inventions that provide an adaptive advantage to our species. This is truly a new frontier whose exploration has just begun."[9]

It is tempting, therefore, to rush full-steam-ahead toward a biological interpretation of the economy and the stock market. We can identify more analogies with biological systems than with physical systems. But we must guard our enthusiasm; this approach is still unfolding, and there are several missing pieces. One of them, according to Farmer, concerns the question of speed: innovation in financial markets is rapid, compared to the slow, random-variation process in biological systems. Because of this, Doyne Farmer believes the time line for market efficiency may still be decades away.

There are some who are dismayed that evolutionary biology cannot make firm predictions. But Darwin never claimed that ability. The Darwinian revolution is very much about how change replaced stasis and, in doing so, gave us a more accurate picture of the behavior of all living things. In her book *The Nature of Economies,* Jane Jacobs captures the essence perfectly: "A living system can be making itself up as it goes along."[10] For that reason alone, I believe that biological systems (stock markets included), unlike physical systems, will never possess a stable mean.

•   ■   •

THE GERMAN PHILOSOPHER IMMANUEL KANT once said there would "never be a Newton of the grass blades." He was wrong. The intellectual revolution caused by Darwin's theory of natural selection is every bit as powerful as Newton's theory of gravitational force.

Indeed, the movement from the mechanical view of the world to a biological view has been called "the second scientific revolution." After three hundred years, the Newtonian world, the mechanized world operating in perfect equilibrium, is now the old science. The old science is about a universe of individual parts, rigid laws, and simple forces. The systems are linear: Change is proportional to the inputs. Small changes end in small results, and large changes make for large results. In the old science, the systems are predictable.

The new science is connected and entangled. In the new science, the systems are nonlinear and unpredictable, with sudden and abrupt changes. Small changes can have large effects while large events may result in small changes. In nonlinear systems, the individual parts interact and exhibit feedback effects that may alter behavior. Complex systems must be studied as a whole, not in individual parts, because the behavior of the system is greater than the sum of the parts.

The old science was concerned with understanding the laws of being. The new science is concerned with the laws of becoming. How ironic it is that biologists, once thought to be stepchildren in science, are now the ones leading us away from the old science into the new, a New Science that is a critical part of the platform for the New Investing.

●　　■　　●

IT SEEMS FAIR TO GIVE CHARLES DARWIN the last word. He was a gifted writer whose scientific observations have become literary masterpieces. One of his best-known passages is the last paragraph in *The Origin of Species,* and it serves as a fitting end to this chapter.

It is interesting to contemplate an entangled bank, clothed with many plants of many kinds, with birds singing on the bushes, with various insects flitting about, and with worms crawling through the damp earth, and to reflect that these elaborately constructed forms, so different from each other, and dependent on each other in so complex a manner, have all been produced by laws acting around us. These laws, taken in the largest sense, being Growth with Reproduction; Inheritance which is almost implied by reproduction; Variability from the indirect and direct action of the external conditions of life, and from use and disuse; a Ratio of Increase so high as to lead to a Struggle for Life, and as a consequence to Natural Selection, entailing Divergence of Character and Extinction of less improved forms. Thus, from the war of nature, from famine and death, the most exalted object which we are capable of conceiving, namely, the production of the higher animals, directly follows. There is grandeur in this view of life, with its several powers, having been originally breathed into a few forms or into one; and that, whilst this planet has gone cycling on according to the fixed law of gravity, from so simple a beginning endless forms most beautiful and most wonderful have been, and are being, evolved.

CHAPTER 4

• • • • • • • • • • • • • • • • • • •

SOCIAL SCIENCES: ANTS, AVALANCHES, AND COMPLEX SYSTEMS

The social sciences seek to study how people function in society, with the ultimate hope of understanding group behavior. When we stop to consider that all the participants in a market constitute a group, it is obvious that until we understand group behavior, we can never fully understand why markets and economies behave as they do.

THROUGHOUT HISTORY, poets, novelists, philosophers, political leaders, and theologians have all submitted ideas about how societies work, but the distinction for social scientists is their recognition of the scientific process. This process, in essence, involves developing a theory (a hypothesis), then testing that theory through controlled, repeatable experiments. This is the same approach used by chemists, physicists, biologists, and all other scientists in their search for answers.

Social scientists, as they work to uncover and explain how human beings form collectives, organize themselves, and interact, have adopted the scientific process, developing theories that lead to the construction of models that can be compared with data collected and thus test and verify those theories. However, because their investigation by definition involves the subjective and unpredictable behavior of human beings, in the social sciences the process is less precise than in the natural sciences, and in many circles the social sciences have not yet reached the same level of scientific acceptance.

Indeed, some have suggested that the lack of maturity in social sciences is directly attributable to the absence of the hard, quantitative results commonly associated with the natural sciences. This is now changing, as immense computer power makes possible the collection of vast amounts of data, but nonetheless there are those who question the validity of attaching the term *science* to the study of social systems. We might say that the social sciences are still waiting for their Isaac Newton.

THE DEVELOPMENT OF THE SOCIAL SCIENCES has followed two distinct paths: a drive for a unified theory, and a move toward narrower specializations. The first approach, largely unsuccessful, was urged by the French philosopher Auguste Comte, who in the mid-nineteenth century called for a new science to take its place alongside astronomy, physics, chemistry, and biology. This new science, which he named sociology, would explain social organization and help guide social planning. Comte saw the study of society as a unified pursuit; society is an indivisible thing, he argued, and so too must be the study of it. But despite Comte's efforts at synthesis, the nineteenth century did not end with a single unified theory of social science but rather the promotion of several distinct specialties, including economics, political science, and anthropology.

Economics was the first discipline to attain the status of a separate study within social science. Some trace the history of modern economics back to 1776, the year that the Scottish economist Adam Smith published his most famous work, *Wealth of Nations*. Considered the founder of economics, Smith was also one of the first to describe its effect on society. He is best known to today's economists for his advocacy of a laissez-faire capitalist system—that is, one free of government interference, including industry regulation and protective tariffs. Smith argued that an economic system works best when it is based solely on its own natural mechanism, what he called the "invisible hand."

Smith believed that division of labor is the cause of increased productivity and, ultimately, wealth for the owners of capital. He was not, however, unaware of the social consequences produced by division of labor: the decline of general skills and craftsmanship, the likely incorporation of women and children into the workforce, and the tendency to divide society into economic classes with opposing interests. He acknowledged that, over time, the owners of capital would seek to limit the wages of labor. Thus was set into motion a countervailing view of economics propounded by Karl Marx and other socialists, that capitalism was but a passing stage of development that would soon be replaced by a more humane economic system based on cooperation, planning, and the common ownership of the means of production.

Given this debate over the interplay of economics and society, it is not surprising that at the same time there was an increasing investigation into the behavior of governments. By the nineteenth century, the role of the state held the same fascination for a group of social scientists, soon called political scientists, as did the impact of capital for economists. These new political scientists were soon investigating the political consequence of Adam Smith's laissez-faire economics. How should the government respond to the new democratic rights of working people while at the same time protecting the private property rights of the owners of capital? Deciding who gets what, when, where, and how became the essence of the new field called political science.

Soon another science took its place alongside economics and politics as a separate discipline within the social sciences: anthropology. From the beginning, anthropology was divided into two classes: physical and cultural. Physical anthropology was chiefly concerned with the evolution of man as a species and with genetic systems such as different races in the world. Cultural anthropology, on the other hand, investigated the social aspects of the many different human institutions, as found in both primitive and contemporary societies. It was here that the science of sociology came into its own. At first it was difficult to separate the identities of cultural anthropologists from the new sociologists, but the distinction was made clearer when sociologists began to limit their inquiry to contemporary societies, leaving the investigation of primitive societies to the anthropologists.

By the twentieth century, sociology had been further separated into social psychology and social biology. Social psychologists studied the ways in which the individual human mind, as well as the collective mind, relates to the social order. They sought to explain how culture affects psychology and, conversely, how collective psychology influences culture. We shall see more about this in the next chapter.

Social biologists, for their part, owed much to Charles Darwin. The increasing academic acceptance and scientific maturity of Darwin's theory of evolution caused several social scientists to make considerable advances promoting a biological view of society. There was no greater champion of this approach than the Yale sociologist William Graham Sumner, who founded an intellectual movement known as Social Darwinism, in which he sought to connect Adam Smith's principle of laissez-faire economics to Charles Darwin's concept of natural selection.

In Sumner's mind, there was a strong connection between the struggle for existence within nature and the struggle for existence within society. He believed the market, just like nature, is in a constant struggle for scarce resources, and that the process of natural selection in humans would inevitably lead to social, political, and moral progress.

After World War II, Social Darwinism all but disappeared from academic debate for almost fifty years. Only recently has the biological concept resurfaced. Several scientists, most notably Edward O. Wilson, have reintroduced the connections between social science and biology into a field of inquiry now called sociobiology. However, most have sought to distance themselves from the implication that natural selection can be a justification for social inequality, which they consider a gross distortion of Darwin's message. Instead, the new sociobiologists are now focusing their energies on the more scientific principles associated with evolution and its connection to social development.

●　■　●

ALL THESE AREAS OF SOCIAL SCIENCE — sociology, political science, economics, and the several subdisciplines within each—are, in one sense, only different platforms from which to think about one large question: how human beings form themselves into groups, or societies, and how those groups behave. The study of political science gives us insight into how people create governments; the study of economics helps us understand how they produce and exchange goods; and so on. Of course each individual simultaneously participates in several groups, and so the larger concern for those who wish to understand human behavior is how the pieces fit together and influence one another.

Although the idea of a unified theory of social science faded in the late nineteenth century, here at the beginning of the twenty-first century there has been a growing interest in what we might think of as a new unified approach. Scientists have now begun to study the behavior of *whole systems*—not only the behavior of individuals and groups but the interactions between them and the ways in which this interaction may in turn influence subsequent behavior. Because of this reciprocal influence, our social system is constantly engaged in a socialization process the consequence of which not only alters our individual behavior but often leads to unexpected group behavior.

Granted, this is a complicated perspective from which to investigate humankind. But man is a complex being, and those who would understand human behavior must find a way to work within the complexity. Fortunately, guidance is at hand, in the scientific area of inquiry known as "complexity theory."

● ■ ●

IN EARLIER CHAPTERS, we have identified economies and stock markets as complex systems (that is, composed of many elements). Many social scientists now start with the same assumption. They recognize that human systems, whether economic, political, or social, are also complex systems. We also know that economies and stock markets are adaptive systems (that is, their behavior constantly changes as individuals in the system interact with other individuals and with the system itself). Here again, sociologists now recognize that a universal trait of all social systems is their adaptability.

From those pioneering scientists now studying complex adaptive systems, we can gain new insights into that great social system called humankind and, by extension, into the functioning of specific systems like the stock market.

One aspect of these systems is the formation process. How do people come together to form complex systems (societal units) and then further organize themselves into some sense of order? This question has led to a new hypothesis that may provide a common framework to describe the behavior of all social systems. It is called the theory of self-organization.

The economist Paul Krugman has begun a systematic inquiry into the theory of self-organization, particularly as it relates to the economy. To illustrate the process of self-organization, he asks us to imagine the city of Los Angeles. Today, we know that Los Angeles is not one homogeneous landscape but a collection of different socioeconomic, racial, and ethnic neighborhoods including Koreatown, Watts, and Beverly Hills. Surrounding the city is a further collection of many distinct business districts. Now each of these distinct spaces was formed not by urban planners drawing lines on a map, but by the spontaneous process of self-organization. Koreans moved to Koreatown to be closer to other Koreans. As the population there increased, still more Koreans were drawn to the neighborhood, and thus a self-organized community also became self-reinforcing. No central controller made this decision for everyone, explains Krugman; the city just spontaneously evolved and organized itself in this fashion.

The evolution of a large city is a relatively simple example of self-organizing and self-reinforcing systems, but we can observe similar behavior in economic systems. Setting aside for the moment the occasional recessions and recoveries caused by exogenous events such as oil shocks or military conflicts, Krugman believes that economic cycles are in large part caused by self-reinforcing effects. During a prosperous period, a self-reinforcing process leads to greater construction and manufacturing until the return on investment begins to decline, at which point an economic slump begins. The slump in itself becomes a self-reinforcing effect, leading to lower production; lower production, in turn, will eventually cause return on investment to increase, which starts the process all over again. Some might argue that the Federal Reserve, by altering interest rates, acts as the central controller to the markets, but as we know, the bond market vigilantes often preempt the Federal Reserve's decision. If we stop and think, we realize that the equity and debt markets have no central controller, and both are excellent examples of self-organizing, self-reinforcing systems.

It is important for us to keep in mind that the theory of self-organization is just that—a theory. Although it appears to be a plausible explanation of how social systems work, there are no models yet built that can test the theory, much less predict its future behavior. In the search for unified theories of how social systems behave, however, the self-organizing theory appears to be a legitimate candidate.

The second characteristic of complex adaptive systems—their adaptivity—is embedded within what is known as the theory of emergence. This refers to the way individual units—be they cells, neurons, or consumers—combine to create something greater than the sum of the parts. Paul Krugman suggests that Adam Smith's "invisible hand" is a perfect example of emergent behavior. Many individuals, all of them trying to satisfy their own material needs, engage in buying and selling with other individuals, thereby creating an emergent structure called a market. The mutual accommodation of its individual units coupled with the self-organizing behavior of the system creates a behavioral whole, an emergent property that transcends its individual units.

Just like the concept of self-organization, emergence is also a theory. However, it appears to be a thoughtful explanation of what actually occurs when individual units come together and organize. Although scientists have had difficulty modeling the phenomenon of self-organization, they have made some progress modeling emergent behavior. One fascinating model is being developed in northern New Mexico.

THE LOS ALAMOS NATIONAL LABORATORY is the largest U.S. Department of Energy laboratory in the country and one of the biggest multidisciplinary research institutions in the world. It covers 43 square miles and employs almost ten thousand people, including physicists, engineers, chemists, biologists, and geoscientists.

Most people know Los Alamos as the facility that developed the first atomic bomb, but today the laboratory's vision has widened and now includes several scientific programs that are directed at preserving and improving the quality of life on earth. One of its newest endeavors is the Symbiotic Intelligence Project (SIP), which studies decision making. The SIP seeks to analyze and understand how people, while using information in a network, solve problems and create new knowledge. In other words, the SIP is seeking to better understand emergent phenomena.

Norman L. Johnson is one of the SIP's original scientists. Although the terminology of emergent phenomena may be new to laypeople, Johnson points out that the experience is commonplace. For thousands of years, societal structures have been able to collectively solve problems that have threatened their very existence.

Self-organized systems, explains Johnson, have three distinct characteristics. First, the complex global behavior occurs by simple connected local processors. In a social system, the local processors are individuals. Second, a solution arises from the diversity of the individual inputs. Third, the functionality of the system, its robustness, is far greater than any one of the individual processors. What particularly excites Johnson are the recent technology advances, specifically the introduction of the Internet and its broad application. He believes that the symbiotic combination of humans and networks (as in the Internet) will generate, in a collective, far better results than any one individual can do acting alone. Johnson envisions an "unprecedented capability in organizational and societal problem solving will result from increased human activity on smart distributed information systems, like the Internet."[1]

One of the great advantages of the Internet is how it helps us manage information; in this, explains Johnson, the Internet has three significant advantages over prior systems. First, it is able to integrate a wide breadth of knowledge compared to other systems whose information was often physically separated. Second, the Internet is able to capture and display depth of information. With digitization, systems are able to produce volumes of data on a single topic without significant additional cost. Third, the Internet is able to process information correctly. As we learn in the next chapter on psychology, communication missteps between individuals sometimes result in the loss of vital information. Information exchanged via the Internet is delivered accurately, in much the same way that books and documents are able to transmit information. It is Johnson's belief that these three advantages, along with the interconnectivity of millions of individuals, will greatly enhance the collective problem-solving ability of self-organized systems.

TO ILLUSTRATE THE PHENOMENON of emergence, let's look in on a familiar social system: an ant colony. Because ants are social insects (they live in colonies, and their behavior is directed to the survival of the colony rather than the survival of any one individual ant), social scientists have long been fascinated by their decision-making process. One of the ant's most interesting behaviors is the process of foraging for food and then determining the shortest path between the found food source and the nest.[2] While walking between the two, ants lay down a pheromone trail that allows them to retrace the path and also shows other ants the location of the new food source.

At the beginning, the search for food is a random process, with ants starting out in many different directions. Once they locate food, they return to the nest, laying down the pheromone trail as they go. But now comes the very sophisticated aspect to collective problem solving: the colony, acting as a whole, is able to select the shortest path. If one ant randomly finds a shorter path between the food source and the nest, its quicker return to the nest intensifies the concentration of pheromone along that path. Other ants tend to choose the path with the strongest concentration of pheromone and hence set off on this newly discovered short path. This increased number of ants along the trail deposits even more pheromone, which further attracts more ants until this path becomes the preferred line. Scientists have been able to demonstrate experimentally that the pheromone-trail behavior of the ant colony solves for the shortest path. In other words, this optimal solution is an emergent property of the collective behavior of the ant colony.

Norman Johnson, who like many is fascinated by ant behavior, set out to test humans' ability to solve collective problems. He constructed a computer version of a maze with countless paths but only a few that are short. The computer simulation consists of two phases: a learning phase and an application phase. In the learning phase, a person explores the maze with no specific knowledge of how to solve the maze until the goal is found. This is identical to the process an ant follows when it begins to look for food. In the application phase, people simply apply what they learned. Johnson discovered that people needed an average of 34.3 steps to solve the maze in the first phase and 12.8 steps in the second phase. Then, to find the collective solution, Johnson combined all the individual solutions and applied the application phase. He found that if at least five people were considered, their collective solution was better than the average individual solution. It took a collective of only twenty to find the very shortest path through the maze, even though they had no global sense of the problem. This collective solution, argues Johnson, is an emergent property of the system.

Although Johnson's maze is a simple problem-solving computer simulation, it does demonstrate emergent behavior. It also leads us to better understand the essential characteristic a self-organizing system must contain in order to produce emergent behavior. That characteristic is diversity. The collective solution, Johnson explains, is robust if the individual contributions to the solution represent a broad diversity of experience in the problem at hand. Interestingly, Johnson discovered that the collective solution is actually degraded if the system is limited to only high-performing people. It appears that the diverse collective is better at adapting to unexpected changes in the structure.[3]

To put this in perspective, Johnson's research suggests that the stock market is more robust when it is composed of a diverse group of agents—some of average intelligence, some below average, and some very smart—than a market singularly composed of smart agents. At first, this discovery appears counterintuitive. Today, we are quick to blame the amateur behavior of individual investors and day traders for the volatile nature of the market. But if Johnson is correct, the diverse participation of all investors, traders, and speculators—smart and dumb alike—should make markets stronger, not weaker. And history supports his thesis: looking back, we know there were plenty of market booms and busts in the days before anyone ever heard of day trading, and institutional investors were disrupting stock markets long before individual investors became active in the system.

Another important insight from Norman Johnson was his discovery that the system, as long as it is adequately diverse, is relatively insensitive to moderate amounts of noise (by which he means any sort of discordant, disruptive activity). To prove the point, Johnson intentionally degraded an individual contribution; he learned his action had no effect on participants' finding the shortest path out of the maze. Even at higher levels of disruption, the collective behavior, after a brief postponement, was able to discover the minimal path. Not until the system reached its highest noise level did the collective decision-making process break down.

We know the stock market was unusually volatile over the last several years of the twentieth century. In 2000, the NASDAQ composite dropped a stunning 10 percent in value in one day, on the heels of several steep drops in the Dow Jones industrial average. Analysts were quick to blame inexperienced investors for the volatility, but according to Johnson's research, the diversity of the players actually helps the market find optimal solutions and is not necessarily the cause of the market's instability. But it is equally clear that the market, from time to time, reaches a critical stress level that ultimately destabilizes the system, which is what happened on April 14, 2000.

● ■ ●

WHEN CATASTROPHES OCCUR, we naturally seek to identify the principal cause so we can avoid another disaster, or at least derive some comfort from knowing what happened. We like it best when we can point to one specific, easily identifiable cause, but that is not always possible. Many scientists believe that large-scale events in biology, geology, and economics are not necessarily the result of a single large event, but rather of the unfolding of many smaller events that create an avalanche-like effect. Per Bak, a Danish physicist, has developed a holistic theory of how systems behave that he calls "self-organized criticality."

According to Bak, large complex systems composed of millions of interacting parts can break down not only because of a single catastrophic event but because a chain reaction of smaller events can lead to a large catastrophe. To illustrate the concept of self-organized criticality, Bak often uses the metaphor of a sand pile. Imagine an apparatus that drops one single grain of sand on a large flat table. Initially, the sand spreads across the table and then begins to form a slight pile. As one grain rests on top of another grain, the pile of sand rises until it forms a gentle slope on each side. Eventually, the pile of sand cannot grow any higher. At this point, sand trickles down the slopes as fast as the grains are added to the top. According to Bak, the sand pile is self-organized in the sense that the pile has formed without anyone placing the individual grains. Each grain of sand in the pile is interlocked in countless combinations. When the pile has reached its highest level, Bak explains, we can say the sand is in a state of criticality. It is just on the verge of becoming unstable.

When one more grain of sand is added to the pile at that point, that single grain of sand can start an avalanche, with sand rolling down the side slope of the pile. Each rolling grain of sand will stop if it happens to fall into a stable position; otherwise it continues to fall and possibly hits other grains of sand that may also be unstable, knocking even more grains farther down the side. The avalanche ceases when all unstable grains have fallen as far as they are going to. If the shape of the pile of sand has flattened from the avalanche, we can say the pile is in a subcritical phase and will remain there until more sand is added, once again raising the sides of the slope.

Per Bak's sand pile metaphor is a powerful tool that helps us understand the behavior of many different systems. In both natural and social systems, we see the same dynamic: the systems become a class of interlocking subsystems that organize themselves to the edge of criticality and in some cases break apart violently, only to reorganize themselves at a later point. Is the stock market such a system? Absolutely, says Per Bak.

In a joint paper with two colleagues titled "Price Variations in a Stock Market with Many Agents," Bak presents his thesis.[4] The three scientists constructed a very simple model that sought to capture the behavior of two types of agents operating in a stock market. They called the two types noise traders and rational agents. With apologies to the authors, I will instead use the more familiar terms of *fundamentalists* and *trend followers*. Trend followers seek to profit from changes in the market by either buying when prices go up or selling when prices go down. Fundamentalists buy and sell not because of the direction of price changes but rather because of the difference between the price of a security and its underlying value. If the value of the stock is higher than the current price, fundamentalists buy shares; if the value is lower than the current price, they sell.

Most of the time, the interplay between trend followers and fundamentalists is somewhat balanced. Buying and selling continue with no discernible change in the overall behavior of the market. We might say the sand pile is growing without any corresponding avalanche effects. But when the stock prices climb, the ratio of trend followers to fundamentalists begins to grow. This makes sense. As prices increase, a larger number of fundamentalists decide to sell and leave the market, and are replaced by a growing number of trend followers who are attracted to rising prices. When the relative number of fundamentalists is small, stock market "bubbles" occur, explains Bak, because prices have moved far above the fair price a fundamentalist would pay. Extending the sand pile metaphor further, as the number of fundamentalists in the market declines and the relative number of trend followers increases, the slope of the sand pile becomes ever steeper, increasing the possibility of an avalanche. Conversely, when the number of fundamentalists is large, market prices typically lock into a trading range defined by the give and take of fundamentalists and trend followers. We might say the base of the sand pile is at a subcritical phase.

The April 14, 2000, sell-off in the NASDAQ and Dow Jones industrial average can be likened to a pretty-good-sized avalanche. We might also assume the meteoric rise in the NASDAQ over the previous year (up 88 percent) meant that the trend followers far outnumbered the fundamentalists. By the end of 1999, the slope of the sand pile was very steep. Then in April, one grain of sand began to roll, and soon the whole side of the pile fell down.

It is important for us to remember at this point that while Per Bak's self-organizing criticality explains the overall behavior of avalanches, it does nothing to explain any one particular avalanche. When we ultimately are able to predict the behavior of individual avalanches, it will not be because of self-organized criticality but some other science yet to be discovered.

That in no way diminishes the significance of Bak's ideas. Indeed, several notable economists acknowledge Per Bak's work on self-organized criticality as a credible explanation for how complex adaptive systems behave, including the Nobel laureate Phil Anderson of Princeton University and Brian Arthur, formerly of Stanford University. Both recognize that self-organizing systems tend to be dominated by unstable fluctuations and that instability has become an unavoidable property of economic systems.

Instability in the stock market is, of course, painfully familiar to everyone involved. It is the treacherous threshold upon which we all too often stub our toes. Surely it would ease our frustration if we understood it better. To get a better fix on the dynamics of instability, we will need to venture back into the social sciences again, this time with the help of a political scientist.

●　　■　　●

DIANA RICHARDS, associate professor of political science at the University of Minnesota, is investigating what causes a complex system of interacting agents to become unstable. Or, in Per Bak's terms, she is trying to determine how a complex system of individuals reaches self-organized criticality.

According to Richards, a complex system necessarily involves the aggregation of a wide number of choices made by the individuals in the system.[5] She calls this "collective choice." Of course, combining all the individual choices does not always result in a straightforward collective choice; nor should we assume that the aggregate choice, which is the sum of individual choices, always leads to a stable outcome. Collective choice, says Richards, occurs when all the agents in the system aggregate information in a way that allows the system to reach a single collective decision. To reach this collective decision, it is not necessary that all the agents hold identical information but that they share a common interpretation of the different choices. Richards believes that this common interpretation, which she calls mutual knowledge, plays a critical role in the stability of all complex systems. The lower is the level of this mutual knowledge, the greater is the likelihood of instability.

Think back for a moment to the Merrill Lynch survey of twenty-three factors (described in Chapter 3) that influence how institutional investors choose stocks. We could say, using Richards's concept, that in any one year the top-ranked choices represent the collective decision of that particular group for that year. But Richards's thesis calls for more than agreement on which factor is number one; she believes that the more important question is whether all the participants interpret all of the possibilities in the same way. Does "earnings per share momentum," for instance, mean the same thing to all the participants? If it does, the system remains stable even if people give it different priority. If it does not, the system's integrity is compromised.

An obvious question at this point is how people select from a collection of choices. According to Richards, if there is no clear favorite, the tendency of the system is to continually cycle over the possibilities. You might think this cyclical outcome would lead to instability, but according to Richards, it need not if the agents share similar mental concepts (that is, mutual knowledge) about the various choices. It is when the agents in the system do *not* have similar concepts about the possible choices that the system is in danger of becoming unstable. And that is clearly the case in the stock market.

If we step back and think about the market, we can readily identify a number of groups that exhibit different mental concepts. We already know that fundamentalists and trend followers possess different meta-models. What about speculators who are interested only in directional changes in the overall market? What about traders and arbitragers? What about venture capitalists and entrepreneurs? And what about gamblers who participate in the market for purposes that best can be described as entertainment? Each of these groups works from a different reality, a different sense of how the market operates and how they should operate within it. In reality, there are many different meta-models at work in the stock market, and if Richards's theory is correct, this all but guarantees periodic instability.

The value of this way of looking at complex systems is that if we know *why* they become unstable, then we have a clear pathway to a solution, to finding ways to reduce overall instability. One implication, Richards says, is that we should be considering the belief structures underlying the various mental concepts, and not the specifics of the choices. Another is to acknowledge that if mutual knowledge fails, the problem may center on how knowledge is transferred in the system. In the next chapter on psychology, we will turn our attention to those two points: how individuals form belief structures and how information is exchanged in the stock market.

•　■　•

AT THIS POINT, we have a fixed compass on how to analyze social systems. Whether they are economic, political, or social, we can say these systems are complex (they have a large number of individual units) and they are adaptive (the individual units adapt their behavior on the basis of the interactions with other units as well as with the overall system). We also recognize that these systems have self-organizing properties and that, once organized, they generate emergent behavior. Finally, we realize that complex adaptive systems are constantly unstable and periodically reach a state of self-organized criticality.

We come to these conclusions by studying a large number of complex adaptive systems across a wide variety of fields, in both the natural and the social sciences. In all our study, we are currently limited to understanding how the systems have behaved so far. We have not made the scientific leap that will enable us to predict future behavior, particularly in complex social systems involving the highly unpredictable units known as human beings. But we may be on the track of something even more valuable.

What separates the study of complex natural systems from complex social systems is the possibility that in social systems we can alter the behavior of their individual units. Whereas we might not be able to change the trajectory of hurricanes or the development of embryos, where groups of people are concerned, we may be able to affect the outcome by influencing how people respond in various situations. To say this another way, although self-organized criticality is an inherent property of all complex adaptive systems, including economic systems, and although some degree of instability is unavoidable, we may be able to alter potential landslides by better understanding what makes criticality inevitable.

CHAPTER 5

•••••••••••••••••••

PSYCHOLOGY: MINDS OF THE MARKETS

Psychology is the science that studies how the human mind works. At first glance it may seem far removed from the world of investing, a world of impersonal balance sheets and income statements, especially since the very mention of psychology so frequently calls up an image of a tortured soul stretched out on the therapist's couch. But mental dysfunction is only one small part of what psychology entails. The word itself means "study of the mind," and thus psychologists are concerned with understanding *all* the workings of the brain—the part that controls cognition (the process of thinking and knowing), as well as the part that controls emotion. This leads them to investigate how we learn, how we think, how we communicate, how we experience emotions, how we process information and make decisions, how we form the core beliefs that guide our behaviors.

All those aspects of the brain's functioning come into play in investing, as the interplay of emotion and cognition leads us to investment decisions both wise and foolish. Understanding that connection—how psychology affects stock prices and market behavior—is what we are about in this chapter. We will examine both the emotional and the cognitive domains of psychology, and how they influence the actions of both individuals and groups. To illuminate the connection, we turn first to the remarks of a very wise person—not a psychologist but an investor with keen insight into investor psychology.

● ■ ●

AMONG THOSE who might rightly be called the greatest investment minds of the twentieth century, no one has ever matched the range of Benjamin Graham. Not only was he a successful investor, he was also a teacher, a writer, and an industry leader. He created and taught the landmark class called Security Analysis at Columbia University, where he met David Dodd, another Columbia Business School professor. Together they wrote *Security Analysis* (1934), the seminal textbook for the investment profession. Years later, Graham wrote the international bestseller *The Intelligent Investor* (1949), and soon afterward he became the chief advocate for organizing a professional society for financial analysts. Today there are more than forty thousand Chartered Financial Analysts worldwide.

In the spring of 1976, Ben Graham, then approaching his eighty-second birthday, was center stage at a seminar sponsored by Donaldson, Lufkin & Jenrette. The investment world was still reeling from the 1973–1974 bear market, and stockbrokers and money managers were eager to learn from this great teacher how they might avoid similar mistakes in the future.

Using a question-and-answer format, Graham and Charles Ellis, the seminar host, covered a wide range of topics. Chief on the minds of most in the audience was what Graham thought about the current level of the stock market. Graham reminded them that throughout history, stock prices have gained in value as their net worth increased by the reinvestment of the company's undistributed earnings. But he didn't stop there. Part of the reason for the 1973–1974 disaster, he said, was that the stock exchange was a "madhouse" and that most investment professionals, although possessing above-average intelligence, lacked an "overall understanding of common stocks."[1]

After the seminar, Ellis and Graham spent some time together, and the conversation continued. The problem with our industry, Graham insisted, is not speculation per se; speculation has always been a part of the market and always will be. Our failure as professionals, he went on, is our continuing inability to distinguish between investment and speculation. If the professionals can't make that distinction, how can individual investors? The greatest danger investors face, Graham warned, is acquiring speculative habits without realizing they have done so. Then they end up with a speculator's return—not a wise move for someone's life savings.[2]

Throughout his career, Graham approached this issue with something like missionary zeal. In *Security Analysis,* he lays out the distinction very plainly: "An investment operation is one which, upon thorough analysis, promises safety of principal and a satisfactory return. Operations not meeting these requirements are speculative."[3] If you are an investor, your decision to buy and sell is based on the underlying economics of the stock you own. If you are a speculator, your decision to buy or sell is based on what you believe about the near-term direction of price. The great economist John Maynard Keynes puts it neatly: "Investment is an activity of forecasting the yield on assets over the life of the asset; ... speculation is the activity of forecasting the psychology of the market."[4]

In *The Intelligent Investor,* Graham sternly takes the investment professionals to task: "We have often said that Wall Street as an institution would be well advised to reinstate this distinction [between investment and speculation] and to emphasize it in all its dealings with the public. Otherwise the stock exchanges may someday be blamed for heavy speculative losses, which those who suffered them had not been properly warned against."[5] That is exactly what happened in 1973 and 1974. And that is undoubtedly why Graham did not hesitate to come down hard on his audience that day: for years they had ignored his teachings and now they were asking him how to get out of this mess.

Ben Graham devoted much of his teaching and writing to getting people to understand the critical distinction between investment and speculation. But his message went much deeper than one of mere definitions. We must all come to terms, he insisted, with the idea that common stocks have both an investment characteristic and a speculative characteristic. That is, we know the direction of stock prices is ultimately determined by the underlying economics but we must also recognize that "most of the time common stocks are subject to irrational and excessive price fluctuations in both directions, as the consequence of the ingrained tendency of most people to speculate or gamble—i.e., to give way to hope, fear and greed."[6] To make that message come alive, Graham created the flamboyant "Mr. Market," the allegorical character who exemplifies the sometimes irrational behavior of all investors.

Mr. Market, Graham explains, is your business partner; you and he own equal shares in a private enterprise. Every day, without fail, Mr. Market offers to buy your interest in the business, or sell you his, at a certain price. The problem is, his quotes are all over the place, for Mr. Market is emotionally unstable. Some days he is cheerful and optimistic, and offers an unreasonably high price for your share of the business. At other times, he is gloomy and depressed, and quotes a very low price. But even if you ignore his offer today, Mr. Market doesn't give up. He will be back again tomorrow with a new one.

The key lesson for investors, Graham warned, is to focus on Mr. Market's pocketbook and not his behavior. If Mr. Market shows up with a foolish offer, you are free to ignore him or take advantage of him, but it will be disastrous if you fall under his spell.

Graham, the consummate teacher, was not trained as a psychologist, and so he would never have framed his remarks in terms of psychology. But in his insistence that investors had failed to understand the difference between speculation and investment, he was talking about an important error in cognition. And in giving us the unpredictable, unstable, unforgettable Mr. Market, he was really warning us against the danger of making investment errors grounded in emotion.

OF COURSE WE ALL REALIZE that Mr. Market is not a single individual. Graham was really talking about the entire collective of people buying and selling, and about the collective behavior that they exhibit. The spell that Mr. Market casts is, in truth, the psychology of mob behavior.

The peculiar effect that crowds exert on individual members had been identified years earlier, most notably by the French sociologist Gustave Le Bon. In his 1895 book, *The Crowd,* Le Bon observed that in a group, individuals who may be very different from one another in every respect are transformed into a unified body with a collective mind that causes its members to behave very differently than they would if each person were acting in isolation. The sentiment of the crowd, as well as its acts, is highly contagious, Le Bon observed, and often causes people to sacrifice their personal interests to the collective interest.

There can be no doubt that the crowd effect is at work in markets. Even before Le Bon, Charles Mackay, in *Extraordinary Popular Delusions and the Madness of Crowds* (1841), attributed speculative bubbles to periodic outbreaks of mass hysteria. Some of the more notorious of those outbreaks include Tulipmania in 1636 and the California Gold Rush in 1840. Today many observers believe that the extreme price changes found at market tops and market bottoms are all crowd related. Thousands upon thousands of individuals, despite the evidence and despite, perhaps, what they would otherwise do if making their decisions in solitude, appear to trample after each other buying stocks that are running up in price or abandoning stocks en masse when prices plunge.

What is behind this craziness? Part of the answer lies at the intersection of economics and psychology, within the field of study known as behavioral finance.

●　■　●

BEHAVIORAL FINANCE SEEKS TO EXPLAIN market inefficiencies by using psychological theories of individual behavior. Its chief concern is understanding the irrationalities that underlie people's decision making about money. Some of these irrationalities are grounded in our emotional responses to money and all that it represents. Some are the result of errors in judgment. Behavioral finance, then, deals with both cognitive and emotional issues.

The combination of money and human nature is endlessly fascinating, and many authors (including myself) have written about behavioral finance in recent years. In this section, therefore, I will merely summarize some of the key concepts and suggest that for a more in-depth discussion you delve into some of the works suggested in the Reading List at the end of the book.

It is generally agreed that the starting point for behavioral finance was 1985. That year, the *Journal of Finance* published two important papers that investigated the impact of psychology on stock prices.

In the first paper, "Does the Stock Market Overreact?" Werner De Bondt and Richard Thaler argued that investors often overreact to new information, no matter whether the news is good or bad. Because of this overreaction, stock prices have a tendency to rise far above a company's economic fundamentals when the news is good and, when the news is bad, to drop to levels far below what a company's economic fundamentals would suggest. As a consequence, the losers become the next winners while the current winners are one step away from losing. The contrarian investment strategy seeks to profit from these psychological overreactions.

The second paper, by Hersh Shefrin and Meir Statman, entitled "The Disposition to Sell Winners Too Early and Ride Losers Too Long: Theory and Evidence," described the disposition effect: the tendency of investors to hold on to their losers far too long, perhaps hoping the stock price will recover to earlier levels, and to sell out their winning stocks too early.

Both papers leaned on the earlier work of two noted psychologists, Amos Tversky and Daniel Kahneman. They were the first to document the irrationalities in decision making and how these cognitive errors become embedded in our systematic way of thinking. In 1979, they published what would become their landmark work, an article in *Econometrica* titled "Prospect Theory: An Analysis of Decision Making under Risk."

Assessing risk tolerance is, of course, of paramount importance to investment professionals, and in this article Tversky and Kahneman developed a framework that clarifies how people make choices in light of the risk of the decision. They documented, through research, that the pain of loss is far more significant to people than the satisfaction of gain, by a factor of 2½ to 1. Making a decision when the outcome is uncertain, people will choose the option that they think has the best chance of *not losing*. For example, given the choice of either (1) accepting a certain loss of $7,500 or (2) taking a 75 percent chance of losing $10,000 and a 25 percent chance of losing nothing, overwhelmingly people choose the second option. Psychologists call this "loss aversion," and it goes a long way toward explaining the sometimes mystifying decisions of investors.

Over the last fifteen years, behavioral finance has continued its exploration into the relationship between psychology and investing. The phenomenon of investor overreaction has been refined through more recent research. Many psychologists now believe that a common response among investors is to overreact to bad news (especially if it is received on a regular and frequent basis) and at the same time react too slowly to good news. Making unreasonable extrapolations from a few bits of negative information is known as "overreaction bias," and it has led more than one adviser to suggest, not altogether in jest, that most investors would be better off if they never opened their monthly statements.

Another aspect of behavioral finance is what some psychologists refer to as mental accounting—our tendency to think of money in different categories, putting our funds into separate mental "accounts," depending on the circumstances. Mental accounting is the reason we are far more willing to gamble with our year-end bonus than our monthly salary, especially if it is higher than anticipated. It is also one further reason why we stubbornly hold on to stocks that are doing badly; the loss doesn't feel like a loss until we sell.

Of all the psychological biases that afflict investors, the most serious may be a tendency toward overconfidence (not to be confused with overreaction). Confidence per se is not a bad trait; it's what helps people achieve great things. But *over*confidence is another matter. Overconfidence can be dangerous when people incorrectly assume they are more qualified to perform a task than they truly are. It is far more common than you might think. In a recent study, participants were asked to assess their own driving skill; 82 percent put themselves in the top 30 percent! In another study, 81 percent of 2,994 new business owners believed their businesses had a 70 percent chance of success while only 39 percent believed other businesses just like their own would succeed.[7]

Investors who are overconfident labor under the belief that they have more knowledge and more ability than the average investor. At first this may seem relatively harmless self-aggrandizement, but in fact the effect is quite serious. One danger with overconfidence is that it increases trading activity. Hoping to cash in on what they consider their superior information, overconfident investors frenetically buy and sell stocks, even though it has been clearly shown that, more often than not, high-turnover strategies underperform buy-and-hold strategies.[8]

Because overconfidence has such enormous potential to lead us into trouble, we would be wise to understand its underlying psychology. It appears that, more than anything else, overconfidence grows from the miscalibration of information—gathering information that is less than complete or not fully accurate, analyzing it inadequately, and giving it false weight. Typically, overconfident investors put too much weight on information they themselves uncover and, because they believe so strongly that they are right, brush aside any information that might suggest they could be wrong.

Thus, if we are to help investors avoid certain disaster, our next step is to study how people gather and interpret information and then use that information to form their beliefs. In other words, how do we understand, and how do we believe? For such big questions, we must look into both domains of psychology—cognition and emotion—for both are involved.

●　■　●

PSYCHOLOGISTS TELL US that our ability to understand abstract or complex ideas depends on carrying in our mind a working model of the phenomena. These mental models represent a real or hypothetical situation, in the same way that an architect's model represents a planned building and that a colorful doodad made of Tinkertoy pieces can represent complicated atomic structures.[9] To understand inflation, for example, we use mental models that represent what inflation means to us—experiencing higher gasoline prices, perhaps, or paying higher wages to our employees.

The first person to propose this thesis was the Scottish psychologist Kenneth Craik. In a short but extraordinary work titled *The Nature of Explanation* (1943), Craik wrote that people are processors of information and that they construct mental models of reality to help anticipate events. With a "small-scale model of external reality and of possible actions" in our head, he believed, we are able to "try out various alternatives, conclude which is the best of them, react to future situations before they arise, utilize the knowledge of past events in dealing with the present and the future, and in every way to react in a much fuller, safer, and more competent manner to the emergencies which [we] face."[10] The great exploration in psychology, said Craik, is to discover how individuals go about constructing these mental models.

Tragically, Craik's life was cut short by a bicycle accident when he was only thirty-one years old. Since then, much of the research on mental models has been led by Philip N. Johnson-Laird. Through a series of controlled experiments examining the ways that people construct mental models, detailed in his book *Mental Models,* Johnson-Laird observed several ways that people perform systematic errors in their thinking.

First, we tend to assume that each model is equiprobable. That is, given a list of mental models, we are more likely to weight all mental models equally in our thoughts than to adjust the potential contribution of each model differently. It can be said that humans are not mentally wired to perform Bayesian inferences. Johnson-Laird also discovered that when people possess a set of mental models about some phenomenon, they often focus on only a few, sometimes only one; obviously, relying on a limited number of mental models can lead to erroneous conclusions. (We will revisit the phenomenon of equally weighted mental models, as well as the theory of using only a limited number of mental models, in our concluding chapter on decision making.) We also learn from Johnson-Laird that mental models typically represent what is true but not what is false. We find it much easier to construct a model of what inflation is than what it is not.

Ongoing research has shown that, overall, our use of mental models is frequently flawed. We construct incomplete representations of the phenomena we are trying to explain. Even when they are accurate, we don't use them properly. We tend to forget details about the models, particularly when some time has passed, and so our models are often unstable. Finally, we have a distressing tendency to create mental models based on superstitions and unwarranted beliefs.

Because mental models enable us to understand abstract ideas, good models are particularly important for investors, many of whom consider the underlying concepts that govern markets and economies dauntingly abstract. And, because mental models determine our actions, we should not be surprised that poorly crafted mental models, built on weak information, lead to poor investment performance.

• ■ •

WHAT DRIVES PEOPLE to accept and act on questionable information? Why, for instance, when it is clear no one has the ability to predict what is going to happen in the stock market in the short run, are investors mesmerized by the predictions of market forecasters? Otherwise intelligent people stop dead in their tracks to hear what forecasters have to say about the market and sometimes even make investment decisions based on these prognostications. What makes these people so gullible? The answer, according to Michael Shermer in *How We Believe,* lies in the power of the belief system.

We must start with the premise, generally accepted by psychologists, that people are pattern-seeking creatures. Indeed, our survival as a species has depended on this ability. Shermer writes, "Those who were best at finding patterns (standing upwind of game animals is bad for the hunt, cow manure is good for the crops) left behind the most offspring [and] we are their descendants."[11] Through the forces of evolution we are hard-wired to seek patterns to explain our world, and those patterns form the foundation of our belief systems, even when they are inherently specious.

Shermer suggests that we can better appreciate the role of the belief system when we think back to the Middle Ages. During this period, 90 percent of the population was illiterate. What little scientific information was available was possessed by only a few—the intellectual elite. Everyone else relied on black magic, sorcery, and monsters to explain the workings of their world. The plague was caused by the misalignment of the stars and planets. The death of a child was caused by vampires or ghouls who lived in caves. A man who saw a shooting star or heard the howl of wolf in the night would be dead by morning.

The Newtonian revolution accompanied by the overall rise of literacy worked to reduce outlandish superstition. Chemistry replaced alchemy. Pascal's math explained bad luck. Social hygiene reduced disease, and improved medicine prolonged life. Overall, we can say the Age of Science worked to reduce errors in thinking and irrational beliefs. But it did not, argues Shermer, eliminate magical thinking entirely. Many athletes maintain bizarre rituals to keep their streak alive. Lottery players rely on astrological signs. Many people are petrified of the number 13, and countless others refuse to break chain letters for fear of dire consequences. Magical thinking invades all people regardless of education, intelligence, race, religion, or nationality.

We were not born in the prehistoric period, argues Shermer, but our minds were built there and we function today largely as we have throughout human history. We still succumb to magical thinking because as pattern-seeking animals we need explanations even for the unexplainable. We distrust chaos and disorder, so we demand answers, even if they are the product of magical rather than rational thinking. That which can be explained scientifically, is. That which cannot is left to magical thinking.

Once I became aware of Shermer's ideas about magical thinking, the attraction of market forecasters began to make sense. We are, through a long process of evolution, acutely uncomfortable and anxious in the face of uncertainty, so much so that we are willing to listen to those who would promise to alleviate that anxiety. Even though we know in the rational part of our minds that market forecasters cannot predict what will happen tomorrow or next week, we *want* to believe they can, because the alternative is too uncomfortable.

●　■　●

REMEMBER THE OBSERVATION at the beginning of this chapter that the study of psychology divides itself into two large domains: emotion and cognition. The crossplay between psychology and investing involves both domains, sometimes at the same time. Up to this point we have been considering individual, separate aspects of human psychology from both domains, and their interplay with investing. We have seen, courtesy of Ben Graham, how we make a serious error of cognition by confusing investing with speculating; from his Mr. Market, we also get a memorable lesson in the investing errors made from emotion. We reminded ourselves of the practically irresistible seduction of crowd behavior, and we reviewed the many foibles of human nature in handling money that exist under the rubric of behavioral finance. We saw how mental models help us grasp abstractions, and how shaky models can produce disappointing investment returns. Finally, we looked back at humanity's proclivity toward finding patterns to explain the world, even if those patterns are based not on actual information but on magical thinking.

We must of necessity discuss these items one at a time, in linear fashion, but we know that in reality things are not nearly so tidy. Nothing is more complex than the human brain, nothing more messy than the actions of human beings. We think we are investing, but we continue to act speculatively. We have a clear plan for what to do with our money, but let us read just one magazine article and we decide to scuttle that plan and do what everyone else is doing instead. We do serious and prolonged research into specific stocks, *and* we listen to the specious advice of so-called expert forecasters. And all this is going on at the same time. This chaotic environment, with so much rumor, miscalculation, and bad information swirling around with the good, has been dubbed "noise" by Fischer Black, a man I consider an extraordinary investment professional.

Black was professor of finance at both the University of Chicago and MIT before joining Goldman Sachs. He is perhaps best remembered in the profession for developing, along with Myron Scholes and Robert Merton, the formula we now use for pricing options, but I remember him most for his presidential address to the American Finance Association in 1986. In his talk, titled simply "Noise," this well-respected academician fearlessly took exception with his academic colleagues and challenged the widely accepted thesis that stock prices are rational. Rather than pure information leading to rational prices, Black believed that most of what is heard in the market is noise, leading to nothing but confusion. Investor confusion, in turn, further escalates the noise level. "Noise," said Black, "is what makes our observations imperfect. Noise gets in the way of keeping observed prices in line with shadow prices or intrinsic values."[12]

Is there a solution for noise in the market? Can we distinguish between noise prices and fundamental prices? The obvious answer is to know the economic fundamentals of your investment so you can rightly observe when prices have moved above or below your company's intrinsic value. It is the same lesson preached by Ben Graham and Warren Buffett. But all too often, deep-rooted psychological issues outweigh this commonsense advice. It is easy to say we should ignore the noise in the market but quite another thing to master the psychological effects of that noise. What investors need is a process that allows them to reduce the noise, which then makes it easier to make the rational decision. That process is nothing more—and nothing less—than accurate communication of information.

● ■ ●

IN JULY 1948, the mathematician Claude E. Shannon published a groundbreaking paper for *The Bell Systems Technical Journal* titled "A Mathematical Theory of Communication." "The fundamental problem of communication," he wrote, "is that of reproducing at one point either exactly or approximately the message selected at another point."[13] In other words, communication theory is very much about getting information, accurately and completely, from point A to point B. It is both an engineering and a psychological challenge.

A communication system consists of five parts:

1. An *information source,* which produces a message or a sequence of messages.
2. A *transmitter,* which operates on the message to produce a signal that can be transmitted over the channel.
3. A *channel,* the medium used to transmit the signal from the transmitter to the receiver.
4. The *receiver,* which reconstructs the message (the inverse operation of the transmitter).
5. The *destination,* the person for whom the message is intended.

What is the communication system of investing? Our information source is the stock market or the economy; both continually produce messages or sequences of messages. The transmitters of information include writers, reporters, company management, brokers, money managers, analysts, and anyone else who is moved to convey information: taxicab drivers, doctors, next-door neighbors. The channel might be television, radio, newspapers, magazines, journals, Web sites, analysts' reports, and all manner of casual conversations. The receiver is a person's mind, the place where the information is processed and reconstructed. The final destination is the investor who takes the reconstructed information and acts on it.

Shannon cautioned that there are several points at which information from the source can be degraded before it reaches its destination. The biggest danger, he warned, is noise in the system, either during delivery over the channel or at either the transmitting or receiving terminal. We should not automatically assume that the transmitters have correctly assembled the information from the source (the market) before the information is placed in the channel. Similarly, the receiver can incorrectly process the information, which can lead to errors at the final destination. We also know that the simultaneous delivery of multiple bits of information over the same channel can raise the noise level.

To overcome noise in a communication system, Shannon recommended that what he called a "correcting device" be placed between the receiver and the destination. This correcting device would take the information from the receiving terminal, separate out the noise, and then reconstruct the messages so the information arrived correctly at its final destination.

Shannon's correction system is a perfect metaphor for how investors should process information. We must mentally place a correcting device in our information channel. The first task for this correcting device is to maintain the integrity of the information coming from the source. The device must filter out incorrect source information and reconfigure the signal if it has become garbled. The process for doing this is within our control. To do so means improving our ability to gather and analyze information and use it to further our understanding—the subject of Chapter 7.

The other side of our correcting device, the side that faces the receiving terminal, is responsible for verifying that the information is properly passed through and accurately received, without the interference of psychological biases. The process for doing this is also within our control, but it is challenging. We must make ourselves aware of all the ways that emotion-based errors and errors in thinking can interfere with good investing decisions, as described in this chapter, and we must be constantly on guard against our own psychological missteps.

●　■　●

IN MODERN FINANCE, a direct line runs from Benjamin Graham to Warren Buffett and Charlie Munger. The man who demanded we figure out the distinction between investing and speculating, and who created Mr. Market to teach us about irrational behavior, would heartily endorse Charlie Munger's no-nonsense approach.

Charlie describes what he does as a "two-track analysis." First, he lays out the known facts and the rational factors that govern the situation under consideration. Then, he tunes his antennae to pick up any signals of subconscious psychological missteps, either his own or those of other players. This is Charlie's version of a correcting device: passing the question through twice, first for rationality and accurate information, then for any hint of what he calls "the psychology of misjudgment." It is exactly the same process all of us—professional money managers and individual investors alike—should employ before making an investment decision. We could all do far worse than follow Charlie's lead.

CHAPTER 6

PHILOSOPHY: A PRAGMATIC VIEW OF INVESTING

Of all the different areas of knowledge surveyed in this book, philosophy is both the easiest and the most difficult. It is the easiest because it deals with familiar issues that affect every single one of us on a daily basis, and every single one of us comes into the world equipped with what we need to consider it: a brain, a heart, and a soul.

It is, at the same time, the most difficult discipline, for one simple reason: it requires us to think. Unlike the sciences, philosophy does not come prepackaged with absolute answers. Whereas many of us find quantum mechanics extremely difficult to learn, for instance, if we are able to master its fundamentals, then we can proceed with confidence that, unless some future science reveals a new truth, we already know the essence of what there is to know. Similarly, once we understand the concepts of natural selection and genetics, we know the essence of evolution. But philosophy has no such absolutes. Whatever truth it holds is inherently personal and individual, and exists only for those who have worked for it.

This is not to say we cannot *study* philosophy. Learning the ideas of the world's great philosophers is the best way—some would say the only way—to achieve clarity about what we ourselves believe. But philosophy, by its very nature, cannot be transferred intact from one person's mind to another's. No matter who first said it, a tenet of philosophy does not exist for us until it passes through the cognitive filter of our own interpretation, experience, and beliefs.

● ■ ●

The word *philosophy* is derived from two Greek words, usually translated as "love" and "wisdom." A philosopher, then, is a person who loves wisdom and is dedicated to the search for meaning. The pursuit of wisdom is an active, unending process of discovery. The true philosopher is filled with the passion to understand, a process that never ends.

In one sense philosophy began with earliest forms of human life, as prehistoric societies struggled to make sense of their world. But as a formal area of study, we can say with reasonable certainty that the field of philosophy began, in the Western world at least, around 600 B.C., when serious-minded people in ancient Greece began to think about the universe in a way that was separate from the dictates of religious beliefs. In the ensuing twenty-five hundred years, the field of philosophy has been peopled by many hundreds of individuals, some well known and others less so, and with almost as many different beliefs and perspectives. *The Oxford Companion to Philosophy,* a comprehensive reference work, comprises more than a thousand pages of listings of individual philosophers, concepts, and related topics. For present purposes, we will quickly reduce this vast body of knowledge down to the working parts that are most relevant to our needs.

Strictly for organizational simplicity, we can separate the study of philosophy into three broad categories. First, critical thinking as it applies to the general nature of the world is called "metaphysics." Physics, we have learned, is the study of physical, tangible objects and forces in nature. It is the study of tables and chairs and their molecular components, of inclined planes and free-falling balls, and the laws of motion that control the sun and the moon. *Metaphysics* means "beyond physics." When philosophers discuss metaphysical questions, they are describing ideas that exist independently from our own space and time. Examples include the concepts of God and the afterlife. These are not tangible events like tables and chairs but rather abstract ideas that exist apart from our natural world. Philosophers who debate metaphysical questions readily concede the existence of the world that surrounds us but disagree about the essential nature and the meaning of that world.

The second body of philosophical inquiry is the investigation of three related areas: aesthetics, ethics, and politics. Aesthetics is the theory of beauty. Philosophers who engage in aesthetic discussions are trying to ascertain what it is that people find beautiful, whether it be in the objects they observe or in the state of mind they achieve. This study of the beautiful should not be thought of as a superficial inquiry, because how we conceive beauty can affect our judgments of what is right and wrong, what is the correct political order, and how people should live. Ethics is the philosophical branch that studies the issues of right and wrong. It asks what is moral and what is immoral, what behavior is appropriate and what behavior is inappropriate. Ethics makes inquiries into the activities people undertake, the judgments they make, the values they hold, and the character they aspire to achieve. Closely connected to the idea of ethics is the philosophy of politics. Whereas ethics investigates what is good or right at the individual level, politics investigates what is good or right at the societal level. Political philosophy is a debate over how societies should be organized, what laws should be passed, and what connections people should have to these societal organizations.

Epistemology, the third body of inquiry, is the branch of philosophy that seeks to understand the limits and nature of knowledge. The term itself comes from two Greek words: *episteme,* meaning "knowledge," and *logos,* which literally means "discourse" and more broadly refers to any kind of study or intellectual investigation. Epistemology, then, is the study of the theory of knowledge. To put it simply, when we make an epistemological inquiry, we are thinking about thinking.

When philosophers think about knowledge, they are trying to discover what kinds of things are knowable, what constitutes knowledge (as opposed to beliefs), how it is acquired (innately or empirically, through experience), and how we can say that we know a thing. They also consider what kinds of knowledge we can have of different things. For example, we have learned that our knowledge of physics is different from our knowledge of biology, which is different from our knowledge of social sciences, which is different from our knowledge of psychology.

In one way or another, all these branches of philosophy touch our lives every day. We all have a view of the world and probably some idea of the world beyond. For this, metaphysics replaces unargued assumptions with a rationally organized investigation into some understanding of the whole world. Likewise, all of us have our own ideas of beauty and waste, of right and wrong, and of justice and injustice. For these issues, the philosophy of aesthetics, ethics, and politics provides a systematic inquiry into the rules and principles individuals and societies should embrace. Lastly, we all have at some point expressed doubts and questioned our own ways of thinking. For those questions, epistemology seeks to clarify the process by which we form our beliefs, and to eliminate confusions that can occur when errors creep into our thinking.

Now, without question, each of these three major bodies of philosophical inquiry is a worthy intellectual pursuit. But in this chapter we will focus solely on epistemology. Although some may argue that socially responsible investing links perfectly to the philosophy of aesthetics, ethics, and politics, I do not wish to debate here the right and wrong of individual companies. Neither do I wish to consider the connection between investing and religion. Although these topics are undoubtedly worthwhile, they are best served by others. I am, however, deeply interested in the epistemological questions. I am interested in learning how the process of thought formation occurs, and how good thinking skills can be acquired.

Thinking is much more than just acquiring knowledge, and the process of thinking can be done badly or well. By learning to think well, we can better avoid confusion, noise, and ambiguities. Not only will we become more aware of possible alternatives, we will be more capable of making reliable arguments. How we think about investing ultimately determines how we do it. If we can consciously adopt an epistemological framework, always considering at some level whether our thinking process is rigorous and cohesive, we can go a long way toward improving our investment results.

• ■ •

ONE OF THE UNDERLYING THEMES that runs throughout this book is the idea that a market is a complex adaptive system and reflects all the characteristics of such a system. Thus far, our study of complex adaptive systems has had a mostly scientific orientation. We have studied market behavior from the point of view of physicists, biologists, social scientists, and psychologists. In that we are trying to uncover the science of complexity, you might think philosophy has very little to offer. But Lee McIntyre, an assistant professor of philosophy at Colgate University, disagrees. He believes that philosophy is a critical variable for understanding complexity and that any investigation of the science of complexity must also address philosophical implications.[1]

The first question McIntyre asks is whether the study of complex adaptive systems is epistemological or ontological in nature. Ontology is best understood as a branch of metaphysics. Ontological questions are questions of being: for example, What is the nature of reality? Now it may be that the nature of reality is so complex we will never be able to understand it. If that is so, our inability to understand is an ontological issue. But it may also be that our inability to understand the nature of reality is caused by our own lack of knowledge about it; that makes it an epistemological issue. Ontological limits are caused by the nature of things; epistemological limits are caused by limited understanding.

Are scientific mysteries an artifact of the nature of things or of our limited understanding of the world? At the beginning of each new scientific exploration, scientists are confronted with the ultimate question: Is the world indeterminable, or are there only hidden, as-yet-undiscovered variables? The study of complex adaptive systems immediately raises that question. We know that these systems, because they are nonlinear, cannot be studied with traditional linear methods. We also know that the emergent properties of these systems all but disappear when they are simplified or reduced into individual parts, which also invalidates reductionist methods of study. Complex adaptive systems must be studied at a level of description that preserves the whole system. "Thus," explains McIntyre, "a central idea behind complexity theory is that there are limits to our knowledge of some systems, even though they are ordered, because we must study this order only at a level of inquiry at which the complexity of the system is ineliminable."[2]

But what is underneath these limits to understanding? Are complex adaptive systems really complex and unexplainable (ontological) or are they complex only because of our limited abilities to understand them (epistemological)? That question is a fundamental issue in philosophy, and it is identical to the one asked more than 350 years ago. Until Newton proposed his laws of planetary motion (epistemological), the workings of nature and the heavens were considered so complex as to be unexplainable (an ontological limitation).

It is McIntyre's belief that complex adaptive systems are not inherently complex but rather appear so only because of our limited descriptive abilities. "Once one accepts that complex systems are only complex as described, there is always the possibility that some alternative description—some *redescription* [italics mine]—of the system will yield regularities that are simpler and can be handled by science," he explains. "If there is order behind complex systems, and if complexity is remediable by alternative descriptions, doesn't it follow that some redescriptions will make that order apparent while others will not?"[3] McIntyre thus asks us to consider that complexity is not an innate feature of the world, but rather a derivative of how we think. To paraphrase the poet Alexander Pope, disorder is nothing more than order misunderstood.

McIntyre points out that the sense of disorder that appears on the surface is less confusing underneath, and that the mandate for scientists is therefore to search for different descriptions that get beneath the surface. This is, if we stop and think for a minute, the very heart of scientific investigation: finding new ways to describe observed phenomena.

Redescription is not, however, the sole province of science. It is also a critical tool for nonscientists who search for understanding. If things remain a mystery, our job then is to shuffle our descriptions and offer redescriptions. Think of it this way: redescriptions are very powerful tools capable of breaking gridlock that sometimes occurs in the pursuit of understanding. I firmly believe, for instance, that one reason we have such difficulty understanding markets is that we have been locked into an equilibrium description of how they should behave. To reach a higher level of understanding, we must remain open-minded to accepting new descriptions of systems that appear complex, whether they be financial markets, social and political systems, or the physical world.

Do not, however, assume that I advocate a kind of intellectual free-for-all. The goal of scientists is to explain nature in descriptive terms that do not violate the basic assumptions of nature itself. The goal of investors is to explain the market in terms that accommodate its basic principles. We cannot slap together any description or combination of descriptions that on the surface appear to offer some legitimate explanation. We cannot create order where there is none. Nature is not so obliging, and neither are markets. Naïve correlations will quickly be dissipated.

With that caveat firmly in place, we are ready to begin an exploration filled with redescriptions. Because this is a chapter on philosophy, we first look for philosophical guideposts that will make our journey more sensible, and we find such a guidepost in the philosophy of pragmatism.

• ■ •

AS A FORMAL BRANCH OF PHILOSOPHY, pragmatism is only one hundred years old; it was first brought to public attention by William James in an 1898 lecture at the University of California, Berkeley. In his lecture, entitled "Philosophical Conceptions and Practical Results," James introduced what he called "the principle of Peirce, the principal of pragmatism." It was a clear homage to his friend and fellow philosopher Charles Sanders Peirce.

Some twenty years earlier, a small group of scientists, philosophers, and other intellectuals in Cambridge, Massachusetts, including James, Peirce, and Oliver Wendell Holmes, had formed themselves into the Metaphysical Club for the purpose of critically discussing metaphysical questions about beliefs and reality. Stimulated by the club discussions, Peirce found himself increasingly moving away from metaphysical abstractions and toward a different way of defining reality. Originally trained as a mathematician, he came to believe that reality is a function not of abstract absolutes but of the practical relationships between entities (he referred to them as symbols or signs, a reflection of his algebraic work).

Through lively discussions at the Metaphysical Club, Peirce refined his theories and eventually came to this proposition: It is through thinking that people resolve doubts and form their beliefs, and their subsequent actions follow from those beliefs and become habits. Therefore, anyone who seeks to determine the true definition of a belief should look not at the belief itself but at the actions that result from it. He called this proposition "pragmatism," a term, he pointed out, with the same root as *practice* or *practical,* thus cementing his view that the meaning of an idea is the same as its practical results. "Our idea of anything," he explained, "is our idea of its sensible effects." In his classic 1878 paper, "How to Make Our Ideas Clear," Peirce continued: "The whole function of thought is to produce habits of action. To develop its meaning, we have, therefore, simply to determine what habits it produces, for what a thing means is simply what habit it involves."[4]

When originally published, "How to Make Our Ideas Clear" caused few ripples outside Peirce's small circle. But another club member, William James, was profoundly influenced by Peirce's ideas, and twenty years later brought them to the attention of the general public, beginning with the Berkeley lecture in 1898.

Peirce, we should point out, was concerned with developing a logical way of solving philosophical problems—specifically, a method for establishing the meaning of things. He intended this concept to be applied principally to scientific inquiry. James, for his part, took Peirce's method and applied it to thinking in general. He moved away from the narrow question of how we establish meaning to the broader questions of both meaning and truth. A belief is true, James said, not because it can stand up to logical scrutiny but rather because holding it puts a person into more useful relations with the world.

Like Peirce, James concluded that philosophers had wasted far too much time debating abstract principles (metaphysical issues) and trying to prove or disprove various philosophical tenets. Instead, he argued, they should ask what practical effects come from holding one philosophical view over another. More bluntly, James asks, in his famous statement, "what is the cash-value" of the belief in terms of a person's practical experience?

James, a popular and charismatic lecturer, soon became much better known than Peirce as the chief proponent of pragmatism. Eventually, Peirce distanced himself from James's work and even gave his own theory a slightly different name: *pragmaticism,* a term he called "too ugly to be kidnapped." In his later years Peirce became an eccentric, poverty-stricken recluse. William James contributed to his financial support and never failed to acknowledge Peirce as the founder of the philosophical movement for which he, James, became famous.

●　■　●

WILLIAM JAMES WAS BORN IN 1842 into a boisterous, unconventional family of intellectuals. His father, Henry James, was a theologian and minor philosopher who educated his children principally by having them sit in on discussions of invited adult guests, and by relentlessly moving the family from one European capital to another in search of intellectual stimulation. William's younger brother, named Henry after their father, became the famous novelist.

As a youngster, William wanted to become a professional artist, but he soon admitted he lacked the level of talent needed for success. At the age of eighteen, he entered the Lawrence Scientific School of Harvard University and then went on earn a medical degree from Harvard Medical School, with a concentration in psychology. He joined the Harvard faculty and attained a significant reputation as a psychologist, highlighted by the 1890 publication of his classic text, *Principles of Psychology*. At the same time he was, as we have seen, devoting more and more of his considerable intellectual gifts to the study of philosophy.

James's perspective was uncommonly broad. He read widely in classical philosophy and maintained lively personal contacts with several contemporary philosophers, particularly Peirce. His training in psychology gave him a fuller understanding of the workings of the human mind than most philosophers enjoyed. He was also captivated by the theory of evolution, which was then still quite new and causing much excitement among scientists in America (Darwin's *Origin of Species* was published about the time James entered Harvard as an undergraduate). Blending all these influences along with his personal reflections, James gradually developed his own style of pragmatism. Because he devoted most of his professional energy to writing and lecturing on the subject, and because both were well received by the public, James became the best-known proponent of this philosophy, and his ideas became accepted as the popular understanding of pragmatism.

To state the matter as simply as possible, pragmatism holds that truth (in statements) and rightness (in actions) are defined by their practical outcomes. An idea or an action is true, and real, and good, if it makes a meaningful difference. To understand something, then, we must ask what difference it makes, what its consequences are. "Truth," James wrote, "is the name of whatever proves itself to be good in the way of belief."[5]

If truth and value are determined by their practical application in the world, then it follows that truth will change as circumstances change and as new discoveries about the world are made. Our understanding of truth evolves. Darwin smiles.

In this, pragmatism is the exact opposite of most earlier schools of philosophic thought, which hold that their version of truth (however they theorize it) is absolute and unchangeable. But James believed that we can never expect to receive absolute proof of anything. Asking, for example, whether God's existence can be proved is a waste of time, because the answer is irrelevant. We need only ask ourselves what difference believing or not believing in God makes in our life. This attitude became central to James's pragmatic approach.

James promulgated his ideas in a series of lectures designed for, and attended by, the general public. He addressed his speeches to a popular audience because he believed that they, not philosophers, were the ultimate authority over philosophical questions. In those pre-television days, such events were quite popular, and James was very well received. His speaking style was dynamic, and his articulate and stylish use of language showed some of the same gifts as his brother, the novelist.

One typical lecture, given in 1907 to a large audience in New York, was entitled "What Pragmatism Means." James began by asking his listeners to observe how science had evolved over the years. When the first laws of mathematics and physics were discovered, he said, people believed they had "deciphered authentically the eternal thoughts of the Almighty" and that such laws were therefore absolute. But as science developed, he continued, it became clear that our basic laws are only approximations, not absolutes. Furthermore the laws themselves had grown in number, with many different rival formulations proposed within each discipline. Scientists, he said, had come to realize that no one theory is the "absolute transcript of reality, but any one of them may from some point of view be useful."[6]

The great use of beliefs, James pointed out, is to help summarize old facts and then lead the way to new ones. After all, he reminded the audience, all our beliefs are man-made. They are a conceptual language we use to write down our observations of nature and as such become the choice of our experience. Thus, he summarized, "ideas (which themselves are but parts of our experience) become true just in so far as they help us to get into satisfactory relation with other parts of our experience."[7]

How do we get from old beliefs to new beliefs? According to James, the process is the same as that followed by any scientist.

> An individual has a stock of old opinions already, but he meets a new experience that puts them to strain. Somebody contradicts them; or in a reflective moment he discovers that they contradict each other; or he hears of facts with which they are incompatible; or desires arise in him which they cease to satisfy. The result is an inward trouble

to which his mind till then had been a stranger, and from which he seeks to escape by modifying his previous mass of opinions. He saves as much of it as he can, for in this matter of belief we are all extreme conservatives. So he tries to change first this opinion, and then that (for they resist change very variously), until at last some idea comes up which he can graft upon the ancient stock with a minimum of disturbance of the latter, some idea that mediates between the stock and the new experience and runs them into one another most felicitously and expediently.[8]

What happens, to summarize James, is that the new idea is adopted while the older truths are preserved with as little disruption as possible. The new truths are simply go-betweens, transition-smoothers, that help us get from one point to the next. "Our thoughts become true," says James, "as they successfully exert their go-between function."[9] A belief is true and has "cash-value" if it helps us get from one place to another. Truth then becomes a verb, not a noun.

So we can say that pragmatism is a process that allows people to navigate an uncertain world without becoming stranded on the desert island of absolutes. Pragmatism has no prejudices, dogmas, or rigid canons. It will entertain any hypothesis and consider any evidence. If you need facts, take the facts. If you need religion, take religion. If you need to experiment, go experiment. "In short, pragmatism widens the field of search for God," says James. "Her only test of probable truth is what works best in the way of leading us."[10]

Pragmatism has been called a uniquely American philosophy. Its heyday (the early part of the twentieth century) coincided with the great westward expansion, and in many ways it echoes the pioneering spirit that we associate with that movement. It also coincided with a time of tremendous economic and industrial expansion in our country, when a sense of optimism and New World success seemed to call for a new philosophy. In more recent times, the essence of pragmatism has often been distorted into an opportunistic approach wherein any means, even corrupt ones, are justified by a satisfactory end. This is not James's intention at all. His foremost concern was with morality; he proposed a philosophical method for living well and honorably with our fellow human beings and our environment.

Pragmatism, in summary, is not a philosophy as much as it is a way of *doing* philosophy. It thrives on open minds, and gleefully invites experimentation. It rejects rigidity and dogma; it welcomes new ideas. It insists that all possibilities should be considered, without prejudice, for important new insights often come disguised as frivolous, even silly notions. It seeks new understanding by redefining old problems. You may recall from the earlier part of this chapter Lee McIntyre's words about the importance of redescribing things we do not understand. Although William James did not use the word, redescription is very much at the heart of his message. We learn by trying new things, by being open to new ideas, by thinking differently. This is how knowledge progresses.

● ■ ●

IN HIS DAY WILLIAM JAMES was the central figure in the pragmatism movement, and he achieved a high level of respect from both his peers and the public at large. He was, in a word, a success as a philosopher. But he is not known to history as a successful money manager. At this point in our review of philosophy, it would be helpful if we could point to a current-day investor and observe how that person has benefitted from the teachings of philosophy, particularly pragmatism. Fortunately, we can.

Bill Miller, portfolio manager of the Legg Mason Value Trust, is considered by many to be the most successful investor of the 1990s. After beating the Standard & Poor's 500-stock index nine years in a row (1991–1999), he was named Morningstar's portfolio manager of the decade. When, in June 1999, *Business Week* profiled "The Heroes of Value Investing," only five people were described.[11] Heading the list were Benjamin Graham and David Dodd, the authors of *Security Analysis*. Next was John Burr Williams, whose *Theory of Investment Value* introduced the dividend-discount model and canonized the definition of *value* as the "discounted present value of future cash flows." The fourth hero of value investing was Warren Buffett, and right after Buffett came Bill Miller.

Bill's pathway to Wall Street was unusual. He graduated from Washington and Lee University in 1972 with majors in economics and European history. In his senior year he took Professor J. Ramsey Martin's class, Philosophy of Language, and it opened up a new world for him. After graduation Bill served several years in Germany as an army intelligence officer. From there he enrolled in the graduate program in philosophy at Johns Hopkins University in Baltimore. Johns Hopkins has deep ties to pragmatism. Charles Sanders Peirce served as a professor there, and John Dewey, a leading pragmatist and contemporary of James, received his doctoral degree in philosophy from there.

As we have learned, pragmatism focuses on outcomes rather than abstract ideals. For the pragmatist, the reliance is not on absolute standards but rather on results—those things that are actually working and that help you reach your goals. Bill spends a great deal of time thinking about investment models but is quick to recognize that any model is highly sensitive to the purposes for which it was constructed.

For example, consider the classic "value stock" strategy built on selecting stocks with a low price-to-earnings ratio, low price to hard book value, and above-average dividend yield. This model was based on academic studies that demonstrated that the strategy could provide above-average market returns. What we have learned about modeling, Bill explains, is that models have a tendency to work for a while and then unexpectedly stop working. Suddenly, the model no longer has an explanatory value, but some people still insist it is an accurate representation of how the world works. How are we to know?

"If you have a correspondence theory of truth," says Bill, "you normally will hold on to that model for a whole lot longer because you believe it captures some deep structure in markets, something that corresponds, in other words, to real things leading to outperformance." This correspondence theory of truth is equivalent to the use of absolutes.

Now contrast this to a pragmatic approach. "If you have a pragmatic theory," Bill continues, "you typically have a shorter trigger to jettison the whole model, but more importantly you will realize that the model is there only to help you do a certain task."[12] As a consequence, Bill is willing to take a look at anything that might help him make better decisions. Of course, he admits, "we are only interested in what works to help us make money."[13]

Bill's success and performance track record are unmatched, but his celebrity has come at a cost. Several critics have denounced Bill's approach, declaring his pragmatic ways are inconsistent with the value-based strategies he purports to use. When Value Trust bought shares in America Online, Dell Computer, and more recently Amazon.com, some critics argued that with those holdings Bill could no longer be considered a value investor. Bill countered he was unquestionably a value investor because he never abandoned Williams's dividend-discount model and definition of value.[14]

This issue is part of a long-standing debate, and the question at its center is highly important: What is the best measure of value? Williams's dividend-discount model is the correct method for determining value; it is what we should think of as the "first-order model." However, many investors shy away from its inherent difficulties.[15] Instead, they drop down one level of explanation and select one of the "second-order models"— perhaps low price-to-earnings ratios, or low price-to-book ratios, or high dividend yields, or some other specific measure—which they rigidly hold up as the only correct approach. In the opposite corner, investors such as Warren Buffett disregard all simple metric explanations of value in favor of the dividend-discount model.

What should the pragmatist do? James would tell us to use what works. A pragmatist would never totally abandon a first-order model, but at the same time he would be willing to look at any second-order model that might further the goal. Bill Miller would argue he has never turned his back on the first-order model, the dividend-discount model, but he does not hesitate to jump from one second-order model to another as it becomes profitable.

The stock market, remember, is a giant discounting mechanism that is constantly repricing stocks. There are occasions when the stocks that offer the greatest discount to the company's value (the dividend-discount model) are the stocks with low price-to-earnings ratios; at other times the greatest discounts can be found in those stocks with high price-to-earnings ratios. No one metric is absolute; none is always right. Pragmatic investors can, and should, apply any second-order model that is fruitful and discard any that are worthless, all without violating the first order.

Remember, James tells us that even "the most violent revolutions in an individual's beliefs leave most of his old order standing." Even when we adopt a new idea, we can still preserve the older ones with minimum modification. From a pragmatist's point of view, it is permissible, even advisable, to search for those explanations that work. "Stretch them enough to make them admit the novelty," James said, "but conceiving in ways as familiar as the case leaves possible."[16]

The philosophic foundation of Bill Miller's success is twofold. First, he quickly recognized the difference between first-order and second-order models, and so he never became a prisoner of the second-order absolutes that have punished so many other investors. Second, he carries his pragmatic investigations far from the field of finance and economics. He is a long-time member of the Santa Fe Institute, which promotes a multidisciplinary approach to studying complex adaptive systems, and currently serves on its board of trustees. The work done at Santa Fe, says Bill, has "helped us let go of simple models and think creatively about the market's complexity."[17]

One of the secrets to Bill's success is his desire to take a Rubik's Cube approach to investing. He enthusiastically examines every issue from every possible angle, from every possible discipline, to get the best possible description—or redescription—of what is going on. Only then does he feel in a position to explain.

To his investigation he brings insights from many fields. He stays current with business and economic developments, of course—no one could achieve Bill's level of investment performance without mastering finance and economics—but he doesn't stop there. He continually studies physics, biology, and social science research, searching for ideas that will help him become a better investor. Most investors read the same newspapers and magazines, they study the same analysts' reports and watch the same television programs. "The only way to do better than somebody else, or more importantly to do better than the market," says Bill, "is to have a way of interpreting the data that is different from other people's. You have to have sources of information that are different and experiences that are different."[18]

That is, in one neat Millerized sentence, a fundamental goal of this book: to help you find different sources of information. When we study the truly great minds in investing, one trait that stands out is the broad reach of their interests. Once your field of vision is widened, you are able to understand more fully what you observe and then use those insights for greater investment success. We live and work in a world in which the pace of change is staggering; just when we think things can't possibly move any faster, the pace once again accelerates. In such a world, successful performance demands flexible thinking. In an environment of rapid change, the flexible mind will always prevail over the rigid and absolute.

The "cash-value" of studying philosophy is very real. Put quite simply, it teaches you to think better. Once you commit yourself to philosophy, you find that you have set yourself on course for critical thinking. You begin to look at situations differently and to approach investing in a different manner. You see more, you understand more. Because you recognize patterns, you are less afraid of sudden changes. With a perpetually open mind that relishes new ideas and knows what to do with them, you are set firmly on the right path.

CHAPTER 7

LITERATURE: READ FOR THOUGHT

Charlie Munger, whose concept of a latticework of mental models inspired this book, is sometimes asked, when he describes his concept to audiences, how a person goes about learning those models. They may use different words to frame their question, but essentially those in the audience are asking, "I certainly understand the value of knowing key ideas from different disciplines and building my own latticework, but I didn't learn any of that in school and I'd be starting from ground zero. Frankly, it seems overwhelming. How do I cultivate the kind of depth and breadth of knowledge that leads to worldly wisdom?"

Charlie is not known for pulling his punches; his answer is blunt. Most people didn't get the right kind of education, he says; too many academic departments are too narrow, too territorial, too self-absorbed with parochial issues to focus on what they should be about, which is helping students become truly educated people. Even earning a degree from a prestigious university is no guarantee that we have acquired what he calls worldly wisdom, or even started on the path toward it.

If that is the case, he says with a smile, then the answer is simple: we must educate ourselves. The key principles, the truly big ideas, are already written down, waiting for us to discover them and make them our own.

The vehicle for doing so is a book—or rather, a whole library of books—supplemented with all the other media both traditional and modern: newspapers, magazines, broadcast commentaries, technical journals, and analysts' reports, to name the most obvious.

It's not merely a question of quantity. No one would be foolish enough to suggest that you try to read everything ever written on physics, biology, or the other areas addressed in this book. Even if you could somehow manage to do so, I'd be willing to wager that, from the sheer volume of ideas, you would end up more confused than enlightened. So we are talking about learning to be discriminating readers: to analyze what you read, to evaluate its worth in the larger picture, and to either reject it or incorporate it into your own latticework of mental models.

Yes, I know … you already have too much to read as it is. But I ask you to consider for a moment whether you might be emphasizing the wrong type of material. I suspect much of what you currently read regularly (the material about which you think "but I *have* to read that") is about adding facts, rather than increasing understanding. In this chapter we are more concerned with the latter than the former. We can all acquire new insights through reading if we perfect the skill of reading thoughtfully. The benefits are profound: Not only will you substantially add to your working knowledge of various fields, you will at the same time sharpen your skill at critical thinking.

In this chapter you will learn ways to analyze a book (or other material) and critically evaluate its contents. That will tell you whether the material has value and it is worth your time to study it in depth. For most of the chapter we will consider how to read books, but using books is merely a convenience, for what we are really learning is a *process*. Books are the most obvious example, but the process, once mastered, can be used with any type of written material, including the more technical material that investors must deal with on a regular basis.

The process is not unlike analyzing a potential investment and has similar goals: to facilitate an informed, clear-headed decision. You will recall that both Charlie Munger and Warren Buffett constantly stress the importance of understanding the fundamentals of any company or industry you invest in. And they mean *real* understanding, not mere data gathering; the sort of understanding that comes only from careful study and intelligent analysis. Thoughtfully choosing investments requires the same mental skills as thoughtfully reading a book.

But what books, on what topics, and in what order? How do we choose, and how can we be sure we are reading appropriately, to make the ideas our own? That is what we shall consider in this chapter: what to read, and how, and why.

Let us start by dropping in on a college campus.

●　■　●

ON FRIDAY EVENINGS, the entire student body of St. John's College in Annapolis, Maryland, along with all the members of the faculty, assemble in the Francis Scott Key auditorium for a formal lecture. The lecture, delivered by a faculty member or an invited speaker, may be about a great book or a famous author or perhaps a topic such as judgment, love, or wisdom. This is, the college wryly notes, the only time its students are lectured to. After the presentation, members of the audience engage the speaker in an extended conversation about the topic, contributing their own comments and asking in-depth questions. For the first half hour, only students may ask questions. The college believes this format serves two important purposes: it reinforces the habit of listening steadily to material that may be unfamiliar, and it gives students an opportunity to polish their public-speaking skills.

But all this on a Friday night, the time usually dedicated to serious partying on most college campuses? Suffice it to say that St. John's is not like most college campuses. In fact, it is unlike any other college in the country.[1] St. John's is a coeducational, four-year liberal arts college known for its Great Books Program. The entire curriculum is devoted to reading and discussing the great books of Western civilization; there are no separate disciplines or departments, and no electives. Over the four years, the Johnnies, as St. John's students are called, will read classic works in literature, philosophy, theology, psychology, science, government, economics, and history, and discuss them intensively in seminars of eighteen to twenty students. In smaller classes, they also study music, the visual arts, languages (Greek in the freshman and sophomore years, French the final two years), mathematics, and laboratory science.

The curriculum design follows an approximate chronological sequence (see the reading list below). In the freshman year, students focus their attention exclusively on the great thinkers of ancient Greece. The second year covers the Roman, medieval, and Renaissance periods, and also includes classical music and poetry. In the third year, students read major works of seventeenth- and eighteenth-century thinkers. Seniors move on to the nineteenth and twentieth centuries.

Through the intensive, formalized process of reading significant works and talking together about them, the students at St. John's receive the kind of broad liberal arts education that Benjamin Franklin promoted 250 years ago, in the famous 1749 pamphlet that we first met in Chapter 1.[2]

In the course of developing this chapter, I talked with several recent St. John's graduates currently working in finance, and their comments were uncannily similar. All of them said that the number-one thing they learned in college was how to be a better thinker, rather than a better trader, investment banker, broker, or analyst—and that being a better thinker invariably made them better at their jobs.[3]

Lee Munson, senior vice president of Prime Charter Ltd., expanded that basic point. "My education at St. John's gave me a sense of perspective, a broader view of the world. It was very clear that to be successful, I would have to consider all the possibilities, not just the tunnel vision you get from standard finance classes. As a trader I rely on the idea that I'm seeing the same pattern over and over again; it may look somewhat different, but it's really all the same thing. I have a much better perspective than people who think this is the first time these things have happened.

"At business school they teach you *things*—formulas, theorems, charts. But that's just punching in numbers in a calculator. What's worse, you learn just one way to do things, and then you can't change your thinking fast enough to keep up with the market. Of course it's important to do all the research, and do it thoroughly, but after that, don't just look to the market or the industry itself to help you with your decisions. Look outside, at the broader picture; that is what lets you think freely. If you don't know how to think, you'll always lose money."

Don Bell, of Goldman Sachs, added: "One other thing I learned at St. John's that was immensely helpful was how to have a meaningful discussion with others on sensitive topics in a constructive fashion, rather than just launching opinions back and forth. You can see that skill develop right in front of you. As freshmen, everyone is so eager to make their own points, they don't really listen; they just wait for someone to take a breath so they can jump in. But by the third and fourth year, we all learned how to listen carefully, to weigh what someone else is saying, and to explain our viewpoint in a respectful, nonconfrontational way. And I use that every day of my life."

Warren Spector, executive vice president of Bear Stearns, added that one of the most significant lessons he learned at St. John's was the importance of going to first sources and forming your own conclusions from them. "Our instructors did not hold themselves up as experts—in fact at St. John's they're called tutors rather than professors—and our classmates weren't experts either. So to defend our arguments, we had to go back and study the original work, the first source. Now in investing I believe the same holds true. Don't rely on so-called experts, like tip sheets, chat rooms, or brokers you don't know anything about, but go back and check the first source, which is the company itself. Dig out your own facts and draw your own conclusions. That's the only way to be confident about your decisions."

●　■　●

READING LIST OF
ST. JOHN'S COLLEGE
• •

FRESHMAN YEAR

Homer: *Iliad, Odyssey*

Aeschylus: *Agamemnon, Libation Bearers, Eumenides, Prometheus Bound*

Sophocles: *Oedipus Rex, Oedipus at Colonus, Antigone, Philoctetes*

Thucydides: *History of the Peloponnesian War*

Euripides: *Hippolytus, Bacchae*

Herodotus: *Histories*

Aristophanes: *Clouds*

Plato: *Meno, Gorgias, Republic, Apology, Crito, Phaedo, Symposium, Parmenides, Theatetus, Sophist, Timaeus, Phaedrus*

Aristotle: *Poetics, Physics, Metaphysics, Nicomachean Ethics, On Generation and Corruption, Politics, Parts of Animals, Generation of Animals*

Euclid: *Elements*

Lucretius: *On the Nature of Things*

Plutarch: "Lycurgus," "Solon"

Nicomachus: *Arithmetic*

Lavoisier: *Elements of Chemistry*

Harvey: *Motion of the Heart and Blood*

Essays by: Archimedes, Fahrenheit, Avogadro, Dalton, Cannizzaro, Virchow, Mariotte, Driesch, Gay-Lussac, Spemann, Stears, J. J. Thompson, Mendeleyev, Berthollet, J. L. Proust

SOPHOMORE YEAR

The Bible

Aristotle: *De Anima, On Interpretation, Prior Analytics, Categories*

Apollonius: *Conics*

Virgil: *Aeneid*

Plutarch: "Caesar," "Cato the Younger"

Epictetus: *Discourses, Manual*

Tacitus: *Annals*

Ptolemy: *Almagest*

Plotinus: *The Enneads*

Augustine: *Confessions*

St. Anselm: *Proslogium*

Aquinas: *Summa Theologica, Summa Contra Gentiles*

Dante: *Divine Comedy*

Chaucer: *Canterbury Tales*

Des Prez: *Mass*

Machiavelli: *The Prince, Discourses*

Copernicus: *On the Revolutions of the Spheres*

Luther: *The Freedom of a Christian*

Rabelais: *Gargantua and Pantagruel*

Palestrina: *Missa Papae Marcelli*

Montaigne: *Essays*

Viete: "Introduction to the Analytical Art"

Bacon: *Novum Organum*

Shakespeare: *Richard II, Henry IV, Henry V, The Tempest, As You Like It, Hamlet, Othello, Macbeth, King Lear, Coriolanus, Sonnets*

Poems by: Marvell, Donne, and other sixteenth- and
     seventeenth-century poets
Descartes: *Geometry, Discourse on Method*
Pascal: *Generation of Conic Sections*
Bach: *St. Matthew Passion,* Inventions
Haydn: Quartets
Mozart: Operas
Beethoven: Sonatas
Schubert: Songs
Stravinsky: *Symphony of Psalms*

JUNIOR YEAR
Cervantes: *Don Quixote*
Galileo: *Two New Sciences*
Hobbes: *Leviathan*
Descartes: *Meditations, Rules for the Direction of the Mind*
Milton: *Paradise Lost*
La Rochefoucauld: *Maximes*
La Fontaine: *Fables*
Pascal: *Pensées*
Huygens: *Treatise on Light, On the Movement of Bodies
     by Impact*
Eliot: *Middlemarch*
Spinoza: *Theological-Political Treatise*
Locke: *Second Treatise of Government*
Racine: *Phaedre*
Newton: *Principia Mathematica*
Kepler: *Epitome IV*

Leibniz: *Monadology, Discourse on Metaphysics,*
    Essay on Dynamics, Philosophical Essays,
    Principles of Nature and Grace

Swift: *Gulliver's Travels*

Hume: *Treatise of Human Nature*

Rousseau: *Social Contract, The Origin of Inequality*

Molière: *The Misanthrope*

Adam Smith: *Wealth of Nations*

Kant: *Critique of Pure Reason, Foundations of the*
    Metaphysics of Morals

Mozart: *Don Giovanni*

Jane Austen: *Pride and Prejudice*

Dedekind: *Essay on the Theory of Numbers*

Essays by: Young, Maxwell, Taylor, Euler, D. Bernoulli

SENIOR YEAR

Articles of Confederation

Declaration of Independence

Constitution of the United States

Supreme Court Opinions

Hamilton, Jay, and Madison: *The Federalist*

Darwin: *Origin of Species*

Hegel: *Phenomenology of Mind,* "Logic"
    (from the *Encyclopedia*)

Lobachevsky: *Theory of Parallels*

Tocqueville: *Democracy in America*

Lincoln: Selected Speeches

Kierkegaard: *Philosophical Fragments, Fear and Trembling*

Wagner: *Tristan and Isolde*

Marx: *Capital, Political and Economic Manuscripts of 1844, The German Ideology*

Dostoyevsky: *Brothers Karamazov*

Tolstoy: *War and Peace*

Melville: *Benito Cereno*

Twain: *Adventures of Huckleberry Finn*

O'Connor: Selected Stories

William James: *Psychology, Briefer Course*

Nietzsche: *Birth of Tragedy, Thus Spake Zarathustra, Beyond Good and Evil*

Freud: *General Introduction to Psychoanalysis*

Valéry: Poems

Booker T. Washington: Selected Writings

Du Bois: *The Souls of Black Folk*

Heidegger: *What Is Philosophy?*

Heisenberg: *The Physical Principles of the Quantum Theory*

Einstein: Selected Papers

Millikan: *The Electron*

Conrad: *Heart of Darkness*

Faulkner: *The Bear*

Poems by: Yeats, T. S. Eliot, Wallace Stevens, Baudelaire, Rimbaud

Essays by: Faraday, J. J. Thomson, Mendel, Minkowski, Rutherford, Davisson, Schrodinger, Bohr, Maxwell, de Broigle, Dreisch, Orsted, Ampère, Boveri, Sutton, Morgan, Beadle & Tatum, Sussman, Watson & Crick, Jacob & Monod, Hardy

AT THIS POINT, I do not wish to argue the advantages and disadvantages of reading great books or about basing a college curriculum on them. Surely no one would be foolish enough to claim there is no value in these great works, and for my part I can hardly imagine anything more intellectually stimulating than working my way through the entire reading list. But debating what is or is not on the list, or the immediate relevance of any particular work, or even the grander issues of what constitutes an education is not what we are about in this chapter. Rather, we are concerned here with the more fundamental and at the same time highly practical question of what we need to do to become better readers, better receptors of ideas, and hence better thinkers.

• ■ •

YOU WILL RECALL FROM CHAPTER 5 that one way through the psychological quicksand threatening our ability to make good investment decisions is communication—the transmittal of accurate and complete information, free of noise. The entire communication chain must be noise-free, starting with the original information being transmitted. Ideally, that information will be accurate and true (otherwise all we are doing is correctly transmitting an error), it will be reasonably relevant to the matter at hand (otherwise we are spinning our wheels), and it will address the underlying question (otherwise we are merely regurgitating data and not increasing insight).

One way to make sure that the original information is accurate and relevant is to apply a correcting device, something we also learned about in Chapter 5. In electronic communications systems, the correcting device is a literal, tangible piece of equipment. For our mental communications systems, a correcting device is whatever cognitive mechanism we can devise to authenticate the information. One very powerful such device—at least for the transmitting end—is the ability to read analytically and think critically.

Once we develop the skills of a discerning reader, we will be able to decide whether what we are reading is worth passing through the communications channel. This is extremely important for those of us involved with investing and finance, for the sheer volume of reading material all but guarantees that some of it will be of marginal value. For simple self-preservation, we must be able to winnow out the good from the not so good.

For us to be able to start the communication chain with good information, we need to develop the skill of discrimination: learning to select, from the sea of information that threatens to drown us, that which will truly add to our knowledge. That is the focus of this chapter: making good choices about what to read, and reading in an intelligent, perceptive way so as to enhance knowledge. And here the students at St. John's give us a very valuable tool.

• ▪ •

IN ADDITION TO THE COMPLETE READING LIST of great books over a four-year period, nearly every St. John's student becomes intimately familiar with one book that is *not* on the list: *How to Read a Book,* by Mortimer J. Adler.[4] Scores of dog-eared, highlighted, margin-scribbled copies circulate among the students, many of whom consider it an indispensable tool for getting the most from their reading. A surprise bestseller when first published in 1940, this remarkable book was revised in 1972 and is still in print, still carefully passed around at St. John's.[5]

There are other books describing a "how to read" system, some more recent than Adler's (see the reading list for this chapter at the end of the book), but I know of none better. My copy of *How to Read a Book* is yellow-highlighted to a fare-thee-well and the margins are filled with notes, arrows, and exclamation points—and every time I open it I find something new. Even though the original concept for Adler's book is sixty years old, the lessons it holds for us as investors are timeless, and I believe it is well worth our time to explore them in depth.

THE CENTRAL PURPOSE FOR READING a book, Adler believes, is to gain understanding. (For the time being, we will set aside the idea of reading for pleasure.) That is not the same as reading for information. The distinction is extremely important, and I believe it is especially important for investors.

Much of what we read each day (unless we are deliberately choosing material outside our primary field, which is a very worthwhile thing to do) is for collecting information. *The Wall Street Journal, Fortune, Forbes, Financial Times, Business Week,* and the other newspapers, magazines, professional journals, and analysts' reports that cross our desks contain new information but not necessarily new insights. When we read this material, we collect more data, but our understanding of the matter does not generally increase. Clearly, information is a prerequisite for enlightenment, but the trick, says Adler, is not to stop at just being informed.

There is a simple way to tell the difference between collecting information and gaining understanding. Any time you read something and find you can easily "get it," chances are you are just cataloging information. But when you come across a work that makes you stop, think, and reread for clarification, chances are this process is increasing your understanding. Using this as a litmus test, think about how much of the reading you have done over the past year was for information and how much was for increased understanding.

Reading that makes you stop and think is the path to greater understanding—not solely because of what you are reading but also because of the process of reflection in which you are engaged. You are learning from your own thinking as well as from the author's ideas. You are making new connections. Adler describes this as the difference between learning by instruction and learning by discovery. It's evident in the satisfaction we feel when we figure out something on our own, instead of being told the answer. Receiving the answer might solve the immediate problem, but discovering the answer by your own investigation has a much more powerful effect on your overall understanding.

The process of moving from understanding less to understanding more is a critical journey for anyone who wishes to gain wisdom. It is not a simple matter of reading one book, setting it aside, and reaching for the next one. Achieving real understanding requires you to work, to think. To the degree that your reading involves subjects that are new to you, you as the reader start out on unequal footing with the writer—the writer knows more about the subject than you do. The more unfamiliar you are with the material, the more effort you will need to overcome this inequality.

Also, some writers are, by their style of writing, simply more difficult to grasp; their works, too, take more effort on our part. Adler likens reading to the relationship between a pitcher and a catcher in baseball. Pitchers, like some writers, can be wild and out of control, which requires the catcher (the reader) to work harder. Although some ideas are controlled and precise, others are much harder to catch. Therefore, if you are going to become a good reader, you will sometimes have to make an extra effort to catch the loosely pitched idea.

To reach a higher level of understanding, therefore, we must learn to read well, and that requires mastering active reading skills. In *How to Read a Book,* Adler teaches us how to teach ourselves to become what he calls active readers, to move our minds and not just our eyes.

ADLER PROPOSES THAT ALL active readers need to keep four fundamental questions in mind:[6]

1. What is the book about as a whole?
2. What is being said in detail?
3. Is the book true, in whole or part?
4. What of it?

No matter how long the material, its format (fiction or non-fiction), or the immediate purpose for reading it (to gain information, to enhance broader knowledge, or for sheer pleasure), you should always be evaluating the material from the perspective of these four fundamental questions if you want to read intelligently.

The heart of Adler's process involves four levels of reading: elementary, inspectional, analytical, and syntopical. Each level is a necessary foundation for the next, and the entire process is cumulative.

Elementary reading is the most basic level, the one we achieve in elementary education. In inspectional reading, the second level, the emphasis is on time. The presumption is that you don't know whether you want to read the book in its entirety, and that your time is scarce. The goal of inspectional reading is to determine, as quickly as possible, what the book is about. It involves a systematic process of what we might call purposeful skimming. In elementary reading, the question is "What does the sentence say?" At the inspectional level, the question is "What is the book about?"

Inspectional reading, in turn, has two levels: prereading and superficial reading. Prereading is a fast review to determine whether a book deserves a more careful reading. First, read the preface. Here the author typically gives a brief explanation of the book, the rationale for writing it, and perhaps an outline of what to expect. Next, look carefully at the table of contents; it will give you a good overview of what the book is about. Then turn to the back and run through the index, looking for familiar as well as unfamiliar terms. This will give you a sense of the book's major topics. You can also learn much about the book from its bibliography. Do you recognize the names of authors referenced, and have you read any of their work?

Next, Adler recommends systematic skimming. Read a few paragraphs here or there, perhaps from a section that discusses a topic you are somewhat familiar with, and then turn to the very end and read the author's summation of the book. This entire exercise, from reading the preface, table of contents, index, and bibliography to systematically skimming, should take at most thirty minutes to an hour. At the end, you should know what the book is about as a whole (Adler's first fundamental question), and that will tell you whether you wish to take your valuable time to read the book.

If you do, Adler suggests a superficial reading, the second level in inspectional reading. Here you will begin to answer the second fundamental question: What is the book about in detail? The goal is to get through the book without getting bogged down in small distractions such as unfamiliar vocabulary. Pay attention to what you understand, and skip over the parts that are difficult. Otherwise the inspectional process will grind down. If you decide the book is worth an analytical read (which we learn about next), there will be ample time then to slow down, learn the new words, and digest unfamiliar subjects. But there is no point in investing your time in an analytical reading until you have determined the book qualifies for the effort.

Inspectional reading requires a high level of concentration. Even though you are skimming the book, you should not let yourself daydream. Stay alert and focus on what you are reading, so that you can comprehend the basics of the material. Adler suggests we adopt the role of a detective, constantly looking for clues that will tell us if the book deserves a deeper examination.

THIS BRINGS US TO ANALYTICAL READING, the third level. It is the most thorough and complete way to absorb a book. "If inspectional reading is the best and most complete reading that is possible given a limited time," says Adler, "then analytical reading is the best and most complete reading that is possible given unlimited time."[7]

Through analytical reading, you will derive (or reinforce) answers to the first two fundamental questions: What is the book about as a whole, and in detail? It will also provide you the most complete answer to the third question: Is the book true?

Analytical reading has three goals: (1) to develop a detailed sense of what the book contains; (2) to interpret the contents by examining the author's own particular point of view on the subject; and (3) to analyze the author's success in presenting that point of view convincingly.

You may find it helpful at first to approach analytical reading the way you would approach assigned reading in a college class. Have a notepad at hand, and make your own outline of the key topics, chapter by chapter. Write down, in your own words, what you deduce is the author's main purpose in writing the book. List what you think are the author's primary arguments, and then compare that list against the outline of contents. Decide for yourself whether the author has fulfilled the original goals, defended the arguments, and convinced you of the main thesis. Ask yourself whether the author seems illogical, or presents material that you know from another source is inaccurate. If something seems incomplete or unsatisfactory, does the author candidly acknowledge that a full answer was not possible, rather than trying to bluff the readers?

After you read several books in this detailed way, you will very likely find that your analytical skills are improving and that you can proceed without the notepad by your side. You will, however, always be concerned with answering these fundamental questions: What is the book about in detail, and is it true? The detailed examination of the book that you perform with analytical reading will also begin to answer the fourth fundamental question: What of it? (That is to say, what is the significance of this material?) A full answer to that question, however, comes only at the fourth level of reading.

THE FOURTH AND HIGHEST LEVEL is what Adler calls syntopical reading, or comparative reading. (We'll use the latter term here, for I believe it more descriptive.) In this level of reading, we are interested in learning about a certain subject, and to do so we compare and contrast the works of several authors rather than focusing on just one work by one author. Adler considers this the most demanding and most complex level of reading. It involves two challenges: first, searching for possible books on the subject; and then deciding, after finding them, which books should be read.

Once you have identified the subject you wish to study, the next step is to construct a bibliography. Depending on the subject, the bibliography might include a few books or many. To read that number of books analytically would take months, maybe years. So comparative readers must use shortcuts, employing a strategy that is not unlike inspectional reading. This involves inspecting each book to ensure it has something important to say about the subject and then discarding less relevant ones. Once you have decided which books to include, you are ready to begin.

The first step in comparative reading is to locate the relevant passages in each book. You are not doing a full analysis of each book individually but finding the important parts of each separate book that relate to what you need to know about. This is a fundamentally different approach from analyzing a book in its entirety. In analytical reading, you accept information from the author as it is given; in comparative reading, your investigation must serve your own needs.

Develop your list of questions, expressed in your own language, and analyze how well the selected books answer those questions. Do not be dismayed if the authors give different answers to your questions, but do take the time to determine the context for each author's answer.

The final step in comparative reading is analyzing the discussion among all the authors. Be careful not to take sides but to let the debate between authors unfold with some objectivity. Of course, perfect objectivity is rarely possible, but the more you can resist jumping to conclusions, the better will be your overall understanding. At the end, you will have answered the last of Adler's fundamental questions: What of it? Is this material important to me, and does it require me to learn more?

To illustrate the process with a relatively light-hearted example, let's say that you are intrigued with the story of Charles Darwin and his discoveries. You want to understand more about the process of evolution as it applies to finance and markets, but you also think it would be interesting to learn about Darwin the man and the events of his life as a scientist. In a sort of mental doodling, without self-editing, you let yourself wonder:

- I know a bit about sailing; wouldn't it be fun to try to imagine a five-year, round-the-world journey on a small boat?
- Whenever I go hiking, I always enjoy the birds; but I never thought about the minor differences between species. What kind of mind would you have to have to notice the shape of the beak and then figure out why that was important?

- I remember what it was like to be young and just starting out in my profession. How did Darwin—whose formal education was in a completely different area (theology)—manage the scrutiny of older and more established scientific colleagues?
- His maternal grandfather was Josiah Wedgwood, the creator of that beautiful tableware. That's interesting. I wonder whether his creative style came from that side of the family.
- He was about to propose a theory that he knew would bring personal animosity and professional scorn; how did he handle it?
- What would Darwin have thought of the uses to which his ideas were put? Would he have supported Social Darwinism, for instance, or rejected it?
- Much of Darwin's theory has been ratified with today's more sophisticated research methods, but some aspects of it have been shown to be inaccurate. What do contemporary scientists think of Darwin?

Convert all your "I wonders" into a list of key questions, and you may come up with something like this:

- I want to know about Darwin's early life and the influences on his intellectual development.
- I want to know about the voyage of the *Beagle* in full, rich detail.
- I want to know how his theories evolved, how they were received by his contemporaries, and how today's scientists view them.

So, you need to explore two types of books: biographies of Darwin, and analyses of his work by current scientists or science writers. You pull together (from the library catalog, Internet resources, bibliographies in other books, and so forth) a list of possibles, and do a brief inspectional reading of each. Those that address your questions stay; those that do not, do not.

Now you are ready to compare the books. (Because you are investigating two sets of questions, you probably have two piles of books. The process is the same for each.) Find the parts of each book that deal with your questions. The authors may use different terminology to discuss the various issues; in that case, you'll have to translate everything into a common vocabulary. Compare what the authors say in those selected passages, factor in whatever you can learn about their own point of view, and gradually you will develop a sense of which books you feel most confident about. Those are the ones that deserve a complete, careful reading.

Don't be surprised if your reading in those books reveals some new ideas about Darwin, new ideas that expand your original list of questions and ultimately lead you to yet more books. That's the fun of it.

LOOKING BACK OVER Adler's complete program, we take note of the connections he has carefully built. Each level of reading is connected to the next, and the process is cumulative. It is obvious that without the basic skills of elementary reading, no one could ever undertake an inspectional reading. We have also learned how important inspectional reading is to analytical reading. Finally, we see that both inspectional and analytical reading are needed in preparing for comparative reading. We cannot hope to reach the highest level of reading until we master the earlier ones.

•   ■   •

IT IS IMPORTANT TO NOTE that the techniques we have discussed thus far apply to nonfiction books, or what Adler calls expository work. (We shall consider fiction a bit later.) Adler defines as *expository* any book that conveys knowledge, and subdivides those books into two categories: practical and theoretical.

Theoretical books are concerned with ideas—history, mathematics, science, and social sciences. Practical books, in contrast, suggest action. Whatever truth is contained within them becomes real only when you take action; merely reading the book is not sufficient. How-to books are the most familiar example. Any book that lists a set of rules or steps that you should follow to reach a goal is a practical book. Of course, many practical books also have a theoretical component. Typically, they first present general principles that are then transformed into action steps.

Practical books are very much about a process—step-by-step rules—and an end result. To analyze a practical book, you must focus on both the set of rules (the means) and the goal (the end). The rules have to make sense to you, and they have to appear doable.

As Adler points out, *How to Read a Book* is a practical book. It has a set of rules and an end result, or goal. When analyzing the book, you would consider first whether the goal is worthwhile, and then whether the rules are the most logical way to reach it. Of course frequently we find ourselves needing to learn about a topic, and we go out in search of books that will provide that information. That is to say, we have already set the goal for ourselves, and now we are searching for the best resources. In that case, comparative reading becomes particularly valuable. To continue with the example of *How to Read a Book,* you would compare several books on the general topic of critical reading, and you might or might not select Adler's book as your guide.

●　■　●

READING A THEORETICAL BOOK is an entirely different matter. Here we are not concerned with rule sets and end results; we simply want to learn something about history, or science, or philosophy, or some other discipline where we believe our knowledge is incomplete. The author's goal is also different: not to provide an action road map but, by explanation and reason, to convey knowledge.

The challenge for us as readers is to receive that knowledge and integrate it into our latticework of mental models. How well we are able to do so is a function of two very separate considerations: the author's ability to explain, and our skills as careful, thoughtful readers. We have little control over the first, other than to discard one particular book in favor of another, but the second is completely within our control.

As we have already learned, our challenge as readers is far greater when the material is unfamiliar to us. For most of us, that challenge is particularly acute in books on science or mathematics, where simply understanding the material can be daunting.

Today most scientists write specifically for other scientists; lay readers are not their first priority.

This is markedly different from scientific writing of one hundred years ago. Even today, those of us who are not scientists can read Newton's *Principia* or Darwin's *Origin of Species* and understand them. Although Newton and Darwin certainly wanted their ideas to reach other scientists, they were especially interested in explaining their thinking to the general public.

Today, this is not universally true. Some scientists and science writers have successfully bridged the gap between deep science and popular reading, but they are in the minority. George Johnson, James Gleick, Richard Dawkins, Mitchell Waldrop, Stephen Jay Gould, and others have written books on science that can be read by the average person. Richard Feynman wrote several books on physics that are accessible for nonphysicists, and Murray Gell-Mann's *The Quark and the Jaguar* manages to deal with physics and complexity without intimidating the rest of us.

For other suggestions, check the listing of contemporary classics, given here. This intriguing list of brilliant science books accessible to general readers was compiled especially for this book by the research department of the Institute for Scientific Information. My request was to select the Top Ten—clearly an agonizing choice for these amazingly knowledgeable researchers.

CONTEMPORARY CLASSICS BY SCIENTISTS ABOUT SCIENCE

●●●●●●●●●●●●●●●●●●●●●●●●●●●●●●●●●●●●

A highly subjective list of the top ten books by scientists (rather than science journalists), published in the last few decades, that epitomize excellence in writing about science, the scientific method, or about the life and work of a scientist. Original publication date is given here; most are available in more recent editions.

Richard Dawkins, *The Selfish Gene.* New York:
  Oxford University Press, 1976.
About evolution and genetics, from the point of view of our genes: we are the vehicle for their survival. Two other well-known books from Dawkins are also recommended: *The Blind Watchmaker* and *Unweaving the Rainbow,* but *Selfish Gene* is probably his most famous work.

Richard P. Feynman, with Ralph Leighton (edited by
  Edward Hutchings), *"Surely You're Joking,
  Mr. Feynman": Adventures of a Curious Character.*
  New York: W.W. Norton, 1984.
Books about the Caltech physicist and Nobel laureate have become a cottage industry, but first read his own words.

Stephen Jay Gould, *The Mismeasure of Man.*
New York: Norton, 1981.
Any book by Gould is worthwhile, but this one on scientific
studies of race and IQ teaches much about scientific bias.

François Jacob, *The Statue Within: An Autobiography.*
New York: Basic Books, 1988.
Elegant, literary, philosophical, this book is an artful de-
scription of a life in science by a French Nobel laureate.

Thomas S. Kuhn, *The Structure of Scientific Revolutions.*
Chicago: University of Chicago Press, 1962.
This influential classic focuses on how science moves, how
scientists react to new ideas.

Roger Penrose, *The Emperor's New Mind: Concerning*
Computers, Minds, and the Laws of Physics.
New York: Oxford University Press, 1989.
This challenging treatise on why machines cannot think is
written from the viewpoint of mathematics and physics.

Oliver Sacks, *The Man Who Mistook His Wife for a Hat*
and Other Clinical Tales. New York: Summit Books,
1985.
A neurologist shows how mental and perceptual abnormali-
ties reveal normal brain function.

Lewis Thomas, *The Lives of a Cell: Notes of a Biology Watcher.* New York: Viking Press, 1974.

These erudite essays cover a wide range of research topics—pheromones, germs, computers, and much more.

James D. Watson, *The Double Helix: A Personal Account of the Discovery of the Structure of DNA.* New York: Atheneum, 1968.

The highly personal story of a stunning discovery by a very young man, this book offers insight into competition among researchers and the importance of priority in science.

Steven Weinberg, *The First Three Minutes: A Modern View of the Origin of the Universe.* New York: Basic Books, 1977.

The physics Nobel laureate dramatically describes how it all began.

Source: Institute for Scientific Information (ISI—Thomson Scientific), Research Department, Philadelphia, PA, 2000.

The authors mentioned here are, unfortunately, exceptions. I regret that I have no easy solutions for those who want to read and understand today's science and math. Unless they studied this material in college and have some familiarity with basic concepts and terminology, too often lay readers are left behind.

READING PHILOSOPHY is similar to all other kinds of expository material in that it requires us to become actively involved in the material by carefully considering Adler's four fundamental questions. But it is also different, in that this detailed thinking is the *only* way we can truly read philosophy. Unlike a work of science, we cannot independently verify whether the book is true. We can only consider whether the writer's ideas ring true to us, in accord with our own consideration of the same questions.

How, then, should we approach the reading of philosophy? First, using Adler's principles, you must do everything you can to uncover the author's perspective, the basic assumptions that undergird his or her ideas. If they are not explicitly stated, you will have to do some detective work. This may mean reading several of the author's works, looking for clues. It may mean learning more about the history and culture of the times. It may mean reading other philosophers who are concerned with the same questions. Next, decide whether the writer adheres to his own assumptions.

Then, try to understand the vocabulary used to describe the questions. This can sometimes be tricky because the words are usually in common language but may have been given special meaning. Finally, and most important, make up your own mind, using common sense and your own observations of the world around you. "It is, indeed, the most distinctive mark of philosophical questions that everyone must answer them for himself," Adler points out. "Taking the opinions of others is not solving them, but evading them."[8]

To illustrate the process, I'll use myself as an example. Chapter 6 of this book is about philosophy, a topic on which I am not particularly knowledgeable. When thinking about how to approach such a vast subject in just one chapter, I first had to educate myself on the basic concepts of philosophy and then determine which might be especially relevant to investors. My first step was to do general overview reading about the discipline of philosophy. (If you turn to the reading list for Chapter 6, at the end of the book, you will see some of the sources I consulted while writing that chapter.)

Then, it happens that at this point I was able to take advantage of a very useful shortcut. I already knew that my colleague Bill Miller, a phenomenally successful fund manager who studied philosophy in graduate school, finds great value in the philosophical school of pragmatism, so I started my detailed search there. (Had I not had that shortcut, I would have simply continued the overview reading and thinking, until I felt I was ready to draw my own conclusions.)

I read several books that deal with pragmatism specifically, including highlights of its most significant practitioners. To learn about the circumstances of William James's life and the times in which he lived, I read a new, well-received biography. I read from collections of James's own writings and also from the works of several other pragmatists. Finally, I gave myself time to sit quietly and review what I had read, thinking it through in the context of some of my own life experiences. As everything I had learned gradually sorted itself out in my mind, I concluded that pragmatism is an area of philosophy that seems to have important lessons for investors.

GENERALLY SPEAKING, the most popular and easily understood expository books can be found in the social sciences. Oftentimes the experiences described in these works are familiar to us all, and we have already formed our beliefs about them. But paradoxically, it is these same beliefs that make reading social science difficult. Don't forget that your goal as a reader is to determine whether the book is true, not whether it supports what you already think. "You must check your opinions at the door," says Adler. "You cannot understand a book if you refuse to hear what it is saying."[9]

When we read the social sciences, it is important that we separate our front-loaded opinions from the author's. Even more important is the technique of comparative reading. People who purchase social science books are most often interested in learning about the topic, not the reputation of any particular author. For this reason, instead of an analytical reading of just one book, it may be more beneficial to complete a comparative reading of several.

LET'S TAKE A MOMENT to put into perspective what we have been learning in this chapter. We start with this irrefutable point: The mental skill of critical analysis is fundamental to success in investing. Perfecting that skill—developing the mind-set of thoughtful, careful analysis—is intimately connected to the skill of thoughtful, careful reading. Each one reinforces the other, in a kind of double feedback loop. Good readers are good thinkers; good thinkers tend to be great readers and in the process learn to be even better thinkers.

So the very *act* of reading critically improves your analytical skills. At the same time, the *content* of what you read adds to your compendium of knowledge, and this is enormously valuable. If you decide to expand your knowledge base by reading in areas outside finance, including some of the other disciplines presented in this book, you are assembling the individual elements to construct your own latticework of mental models.

Or, to put the matter more directly, learning to be a careful reader has two enormous benefits to investors: it makes you smarter, in an overall sense; and it makes you see the value of developing a critical mind-set, not necessarily taking information at face value.

This critical mind-set, in turn, has two aspects that relate to the reading process: (1) evaluate the facts, and (2) separate fact from opinion. To see the process at work, let us briefly consider analysts' reports. I chose these reports as a specific example, because we all spend so much time reading them, but of course the general approach can be, and should be, used universally.

First, look at the facts in the report. It is not unknown for analysts to make ordinary mistakes in their math. That's a simple way to start double-checking facts. Then look at other facts in the report, and think of ways that you could independently verify them—perhaps by reading the company's own material, by comparing the facts against those in an independent source such as *Value Line,* or by comparing the report against similar reports by other analysts.

Then, consciously try to discern how much of what you're reading is fact and how much is opinion. If you have already found that some of the facts are shaky, that's a good clue that much of what you're reading might be opinion. But even if the facts are correct, it's quite possible that much of the other commentary is one person's opinion. Then you must stop and think about what is behind that opinion. Is there some vested interest at work? Does the analyst have a long-standing personal bias that creeps in? Has the analyst's opinion changed from opinions expressed in the prior reports, and if so, is there a legitimate reason for the change? Every time you read a report in this fashion, you are perfecting your critical-thinking skills.

● ■ ●

SO FAR WE HAVE BEEN LEARNING about doing a careful reading of expository works, but knowledge, insight, and wisdom are not limited to works of nonfiction. Novels, poetry, essays, plays, short stories, even so-called popular fiction can nurture and replenish our understanding of the world we live in.

Noting that they appeal more to our imagination than to our intellect, Adler puts all these types of books under the all-inclusive label of imaginative literature. Although in a very real sense the four fundamental questions apply with equal significance to all kinds of books, reading imaginative material is, Adler believes, far more difficult than reading expository books.

Expository books convey knowledge, he explains. When we are reading them, our goal is to determine their truth. Imaginative books, on the other hand, convey an experience. The beauty of a book relates to that experience. However, this experience is highly subjective, and therefore impossible to analyze. Our challenge as readers is to welcome this experience, to open wide our senses and our imagination. "Don't try to resist the effect that a work of imaginative literature has on you," says Adler. "Let it do whatever work it wants to do."[10]

To gain the riches from imaginative literature takes somewhat different skills from those used in reading expository books. For starters, realize that fiction writers use language differently. Multiple metaphors, shades of meaning, convey between the lines more than is stated explicitly; the entire story thus says more than the sum of its individual words. Our investigation of the truth of the work is also different. In an expository work, technical errors can diminish our confidence in the book. But in a work of fiction, whether the novelist depicts the characters' actions and emotions in a way that seems believable is far more important than whether specific technical details are correct.

In other ways, however, critically reading fiction is like critically reading nonfiction. You must still attend to the content, by understanding the characters and their relationships. You must still find the author's main points, by fully inhabiting the imaginary world of the novel. You must still follow the author's "argument," by allowing yourself to experience what the characters experience. In the end, however, the basic question is not whether you agree or disagree with the book, but whether you do or not like it—and why.

The more practical-minded among you may be wondering what investors can learn from imaginative literature. If it doesn't add any new insights about investing, why allocate your valuable time to it? My answer is simple: because we learn from experiences—and not just our own. Just as we learn from our daily experiences how to become better mates, parents, citizens, and investors, so too can we learn from the fictional experiences that fine writers place in our imagination. In this regard, imaginative literature can teach us as well as please us.

Have you ever found, when reading a work of fiction or poetry, that you are stopped cold by a sentence that perfectly expresses something you have felt but never been able to put so clearly into words? The thought is not new, but suddenly it seems stronger and more real. That recognition of truth can be as strong and sudden as a shot of electric current, and the insight you gain will stay with you. This is the power of imaginative literature: it helps us know what we know, feel what we feel, believe what we believe.

Anyone who has read the work of Shakespeare has learned much about human nature while also being thrilled by the beauty and drama of the words the characters speak. The great poets teach us about love, life, and death. Nature essayists lead us to thinking about our role in the earth's ecosystem. Modern novelists and playwrights challenge us to consider the great and awful issues of our day, while at the same time entertaining us.

This is not to say that only "serious" fiction has anything to teach us. Even works that we read mostly for entertainment can give us new ideas, influence our worldview, or show us a better way of doing things. To use a highly personal example, I am very fond of the mysteries of Sherlock Holmes. I read them for pleasure, but along the way I learn. Holmes's methods of solving mysteries have taught me some new ways of thinking about investing.

Whereas the bumbling inspectors from Scotland Yard are always rushing to conclusions, Holmes resists the temptation. In

"The Valley of Fear," for instance, Holmes warns a young inspector hot on the trail of Professor Moriarity, "The temptation to form premature theories upon insufficient data is the bane of our profession."

In "A Scandal of Bohemia," a puzzled Dr. Watson asks, "What do you imagine that it means?"

Holmes replies, "I have no data yet. It is a capital mistake to theorize before one has data. Insensibly one begins to twist facts to suit theories, instead of theories to suit facts."

Can you imagine a more succinct description of careful analysis?

Now it is true that reading Sherlock Holmes has never directly helped me pick any particular stock, but I am certain that Conan Doyle's stories have made me a better investor.

● ■ ●

READING IS GOOD FOR THE MIND. Even if you were fortunate enough to have the sort of broad education advocated by Ben Franklin and pursued at institutions like St. John's College, you will want to continue reading throughout your life. Exploring challenging ideas keeps your mind stimulated, open, and alive. And if your education gave you specific and "practical" knowledge but not broad understanding, then it is up to you to do the rest—to fill in the knowledge your education did not provide. In either case, the process is easier, and more fruitful, if you learn the skills of an intelligent, analytical reader.

I wish I could guarantee that this approach to reading will automatically give you Charlie Munger's worldly wisdom. It will not. By itself, reading is insufficient. You must put yourself—

your own good brain and some of your soul—into the process, by reflecting on what you read. Indeed, the harder you work to understand and absorb the material, the more deeply embedded it becomes. As Charlie himself puts it, "Good literature makes [you] reach a little. Then it works better. If you've reached for it, the idea's pounded in better."[11]

But if you are still skeptical about all this, and worried about taking on even more reading than you already do, especially reading that you fear will be too difficult, listen once more to Charlie:

"I believe in ... mastering the best that other people have figured out, [rather than] sitting down and trying to dream it up yourself.... You won't find it that hard if you go at it Darwinlike, step by step with curious persistence. You'll be amazed at how good you can get.... It's a huge mistake not to absorb elementary worldly wisdom....Your life will be enriched—not only financially but in a host of other ways—if you do."[12]

DECISION MAKING

A t 6:30 P.M. on a Friday night in May 2000, the seminar "Beyond Equilibrium and Efficiency" reconvened in the Noyce Conference Room at the Santa Fe Institute.[1] The three-day seminar, organized by Doyne Farmer, McKinsey Research Professor at the institute, and John Geanakoplos of the Cowles Foundation at Yale, was designed to gather ideas about market behavior and investing. In attendance was a diverse group of physicists, economists, finance professors, and money managers, including some of the best financial minds in the world.

The debate that night, entitled "Are Markets Efficient?" was moderated by Bill Miller, president of Legg Mason Funds Management and portfolio manager of the Legg Mason Value Trust. To set the stage, Bill began by summarizing the major points presented at the seminar so far. He pointed out that both Richard Roll (UCLA) and Steve Ross (MIT) had presented credible evidence of the market's ability to set prices efficiently. He also noted the presentations of Richard Thaler (University of Chicago), Robert Shiller (Cowles Foundation at Yale University), and Franco Modigliani (MIT), who argued convincingly that individuals, when investing, continually make irrational decisions. So we are left with a puzzle, said Bill. Investors and traders in the market are not rational, but prices in the market are efficient. How can this be?

One possible explanation is the emergent quality of collective behavior, illustrated in Norman Johnson's theoretical maze (described in Chapter 4). Because the market is composed of a diverse group of agents, some below average, others average, and a few above average, it is possible that the market's prices are the optimal outcome, the emergent property of a diverse system.

At this point in the debate, Bill contributed his own opinion. He believes, he said, that markets are directionally efficient, meaning that today's prices reflect what is currently known about the future direction of the market. Of course, something totally unexpected can occur tomorrow that will change the direction of the market, and there are always some people who will alter their bets based on what they think will happen, but in general, market prices reflect all the news that is currently available.

However, Bill continued, some people believe the market is cross-sectionally *in*efficient, meaning that the market will sometimes price individual securities incorrectly relative to others. In other words, the market as a whole is accurately priced, but its individual pieces sometimes get mispriced. Looking within one industry, you might find one company at one price and a very similar company with a dramatically different price. There can be two reasons for this, and they sometimes occur simultaneously. One is that investors are often pushed and pulled by emotion, and as a result make errors in judgment. The other is insufficient analysis. Most people use simple metric models that do not uncover the real intrinsic value of businesses; at best they give only a superficial view of a company's value.

That combination—emotional missteps plus inadequate security analysis—produces occasional opportunities to profit from the market's mispricing of individual securities. This, Miller believes, is why some portfolio managers have been able to achieve above-average performance.

Taking a slightly different tack during the debate, Roll maintained that the market's efficiency was not necessarily a result of the rational expectations theory but was more closely tied to the intense level of competition in the marketplace. Yes, people can be irrational, and yes, prices can sometimes diverge from intrinsic value; but the fierce competition among traders, arbitragers, and other investors who behave like sharks swimming in the market's waters quickly bites off any pricing inefficiency that is bobbing on the surface. Roll suggested we should remove the word *efficient* from modern portfolio theory and replace it with the word *competitive*. He said he would describe the market as being 98 percent efficient and 2 percent inefficient. That is, 98 percent of the market's efficient pricing is set by the competitive nature of the participants, which leaves only a small 2 percent of the marketplace for the exceptional and talented active managers to exploit.

Now a competitive market, Roll continued, does not mean that all people do equally well. Farming is competitive, he pointed out, but not all farmers make the same profit margin. The competitive nature of the market simply means that if you don't come to investing with some exceptional talent, you are going to be in trouble. "There are no gifts for the marginal investor," he said.

Steve Ross of MIT added, "The value of any investment strategy that uses information set at the surface of the market is the value of the current investment strategy." In other words, he went on, "you cannot earn an excess return unless you obtain information that is not already discounted in the market."

The finance practitioners in the audience nodded in agreement. The proprietary traders at Goldman Sachs and Morgan Stanley both confessed that the "easy pickings" seem to be fewer and fewer. Norman Packard, who runs neural networks on global computers at Prediction Company, was quick to point out that inefficiencies still appear but they last for only a short period; furthermore, he added, it has become increasingly difficult to get a lot of money into a position to then profit from the market's mispricing. Sandy Grossman, who taught economics for fifteen years at Princeton and the University of Pennsylvania and then went on to make a fortune as a trader at Quantitative Financial Strategies, was even more blunt. "You shouldn't be able to earn rents [just] by doing simple arithmetic." In his view "rents," which is just another word for "excess profits," are not available for those investors who are not willing to work hard.

The behavior of most investors, Grossman said, reminded him of an old joke. It seems a certain gentleman, after one drink too many at the local tavern, was carefully making his way home late at night. Walking down the middle of the street, he tripped and fell, and his key ring flew out of his hand. He picked himself up, walked over to the lamppost on the sidewalk, and began to look for his lost keys. A cop walking the beat, who had been watching the whole time, sauntered over.

"What are you doing?" the patrolman asked.

"Well, sir, I am looking for my keys."

"Yeah," said the cop, "but you lost them over there. Why are you looking for them over here?"

The man turned and said with a sly smile, "Because this is where the light is."

Investing, said Grossman, has become very much about looking for profits under the lamppost; once they are found, investors quickly snatch them up. "Those people who profit in the market," he went on, "are those people who are able to identify the anomalies not yet seen by the market."

There were some in the audience, the scientists in particular, who argued loudly that the only place the drunk should ever look for his keys is under the lamppost, even if there is but a small chance the keys are there, for the simple reason that there is probably no chance he will ever find his keys by roaming in the dark.[2] In fact, they argued, the advancement of science has principally occurred because scientists have focused their attention under the lights rather than groping in the dark. But investing, we all know, is slightly different.

Let's imagine the stock market not as a single lamppost on a street corner but as a parking lot full of one hundred lampposts spread across a vast open space. The parking lot is also full of investors, all huddled under different lights waiting for the keys (profits) to appear. When someone finds the keys, everyone else hears the squeals of excitement and they all rush to that one spot. Sometimes the keys appear on one side of the parking lot, then the other side; now in one corner, then the opposite corner; and so on. There appears to be no discernible pattern to when and where the keys will be discovered, but when they are, there will be plenty of investors waiting there to pick them up and many more investors running over from different lampposts.

By the end of the evening's debate, a number of people held steadfastly to their view of market efficiency; an equal number still believed the markets were largely inefficient. However, most agreed the markets were in fact highly competitive. In the short run, Bill said in conclusion, there appears to be no easy way to profit from the short-term game of finding the keys. There are some nimble traders and people with high-powered computers who can get a jump-start on most others. But for the vast majority of people, there just doesn't appear to be any easy way to get "rents" out of the market in a short period of time. On the other hand, said Bill, for people who are willing to play the game of "finding the keys" in a slightly different way, there are still profitable opportunities available.

At the seminar, it was universally agreed that it was practically impossible to find excess returns in the market by using simple approaches. Even if someone discovered a rather simple tool to predict stock price behavior, the competitive nature of the market would quickly arbitrage the profit potential away. So if the simple and obvious approaches are the strategies most often neutralized by the competitive forces of the market, what kind of search strategy should investors employ? In this case, Bill Miller concludes, the optimal long-term strategy for investors is to look for the keys in the dark.

● ■ ●

TO THINK ABOUT INVESTING DIFFERENTLY (looking for the keys in the dark) requires us to think creatively. It requires a new and innovative approach to absorbing information and building mental models. You will recall from Chapter 1 that to construct a new latticework of mental models, we must first learn to think in multidisciplinary terms and to collect (or teach ourselves) fundamental ideas from several disciplines, and then we must be able to link by metaphor what we have learned back to the investing world. Metaphor is the device for moving from areas we know and understand to new areas we don't know much about. A general awareness of the fundamentals of various disciplines, coupled with the ability to think metaphorically, is critical to effective model building.

The art of model building depends on our skill at constructing and then using building blocks.[3] Think of the classic children's toy, Lincoln Logs. To build a model of a cabin, children construct, using the various logs, a replica of what they think a log cabin looks like. Now, the set comes with many different logs. Some are short and some are long; some are used for connecting the roof, others are used to frame doors and windows. To build a good log cabin, the builder has to combine the logs together in such a way as to create a good model.

Constructing an effective model for investing is very similar to building a log cabin. We have, throughout this book, provided a number of different building blocks. Good model building is very much about combining the building blocks in a skillful, artful way. Properly combined, these building blocks will give you a reasonable model of how markets work and, I hope, add some insight that will help you become a better investor. Now what we can quickly appreciate is that if you have only a couple of building blocks, it will be very difficult to construct an exact model of a log cabin. This is also true in investing. If you possess only a few building blocks, how will you ever be able to construct a useful model?

The first rule in building an effective model, then, is to start with enough building blocks. To build our all-encompassing model of the market—a meta-model, if you will—we will use as building blocks the various mental models described in this book, the key ideas taken from individual disciplines. After we have collected enough building blocks, we can start to assemble them into a working model.

One critical difference between building a model of a log cabin and building a model of market behavior is that our investing model must be dynamic. It must have the ability to change as the circumstances of the market change. As we have already discovered, the building blocks of fifty years ago are no longer relevant, because the market, like a biological organism, has evolved.

A model that changes shape as its environment changes may be difficult to envision. To get a sense of how that could work, imagine a flight simulator. The great advantage of a simulator is that it allows pilots to train and perfect their skills under different scenarios without the risk of actually crashing the plane. Pilots learn to fly at night, in bad weather, or when the plane is experiencing mechanical difficulties. Each time they perform a simulation, they must construct a different flying model that will allow them to fly and land safely. Each one of those models may contain similar building blocks but assembled in a different sequence; the pilot is learning which building blocks to emphasize for each of the scenarios.

The pilot is also learning to recognize patterns and extrapolate information from them to make quick decisions. When a certain set of conditions presents itself, the pilot must be able to recognize an underlying pattern and to pull from it a useful idea. Thinking faster than I can write it or you can read it, the pilot's mental process goes something like this: I haven't seen this exact situation before but I saw something like it, and I know what worked in that earlier case, so I'll start there and modify it as I go along.

Building an effective model for investing is very similar to operating a flight simulator. Because we know the environment is going to change continually, we must be in a position to shift the building blocks to construct different models. Pragmatically speaking, we are searching for the right combination of building blocks that best describes the current environment. Ultimately, when you have discovered the right building blocks for each scenario, you have built up experiences that in turn enable you to recognize patterns and make the correct decisions.

One thing to remember is that effective decision making is very much about weighting the right building blocks, putting the building blocks in some hierarchical structure. Of course we may never fully know what all the optimal building blocks are, but we can put into place a process for improving what we already have. If we have a sufficient number of building blocks, then model building becomes very much about reweighting and recombining them in different circumstances.

One thing we know from recent research by John Holland and other scientists (see Chapter 1) is that people are more likely to change the weightings of their existing building blocks than to spend any time discovering new ones. And that is a mistake. We must, argues Holland, find a way to use productively what we already know and at the same time actively search for new knowledge—or, as Holland adroitly phrases it, we must strike a balance between exploitation and exploration. When our model reveals readily available profits, of course we should intensely exploit the market's inefficiency. But we should *never* stop exploring for new building blocks.

Although the greatest number of ants in a colony will follow the most intense pheromone trail to a food source, there are always some ants that are randomly seeking the next food source. When Native Americans were sent out to hunt, most of those in the party would return to proven hunting grounds. However, a few in the tribe, directed by a medicine man rolling spirit bones, were sent in different directions to find new herds. The same was true of Norwegian fishermen. Each day most of the ships in the fleet returned to the same spot where the previous day's catch had yielded the greatest bounty, but a few vessels were also sent in random directions to locate the next school of fish. As investors, we too must strike a balance between exploiting what is most obvious while allocating some mental energy to exploring new possibilities.

By recombining our existing building blocks, we are in fact learning and adapting to a changing environment. Think back for a moment to the descriptions of neural networks and the theory of connectionism in Chapter 1. It will be immediately obvious to you that by choosing and then recombining building blocks, what we are doing is creating our own neural network, our own connectionist model.

The process is similar to genetic crossover that occurs in biological evolution. Indeed, biologists agree that genetic crossover is chiefly responsible for evolution. Similarly, the constant recombination of our existing mental building blocks will, over time, be responsible for the greatest amount of investment progress. However, there are occasions when a new and rare discovery opens up new opportunities for investors. In much the same way that a mutation can accelerate the evolutionary process, so too can newfound ideas speed us along in our understanding of how markets and investing work. If you are able to discover a new building block, you have the potential to add another level to your model of understanding.

It's important to understand that you have the opportunity to discover many new things and add new building blocks to your mental models *without ever taking undue risk*. You can throw a lot of new theories and ideas into your thinking mix, assemble them into a model, and, like a pilot in a flight simulator, try them out in the marketplace. If the new building blocks prove useful, then keep them and give them appropriate weight. But if they appear to add no value, you simply store them away and draw them up again some day in the future.

But remember, none of this will happen if you conclude that you already know enough. *Never* stop discovering new building blocks. When a corporation cuts its research and development budget to focus on the here and now, that may produce greater profits in the short term, but more likely it places the company in competitive jeopardy at some point in the future. Likewise, if we stop exploring for new ideas, we may still be able to navigate the stock market for a period of time, but most likely we are putting ourselves at a disadvantage for tomorrow's changing environment.

● ■ ●

AT THE CENTER of the University of Pennsylvania campus, where Locust Walk crosses the 37th Street walkway, there is a life-size bronze statue of Benjamin Franklin sitting on a park bench. He wears a ruffled shirt and knickers, a long coat and vest, and square-buckled shoes. A pair of round bifocals sits on the very tip of his nose, and he is reading a copy of *The Pennsyl-*

vania Gazette. Of the forty-one statues of Benjamin Franklin in Philadelphia, this one, designed by George W. Lundeen, is by far my favorite. The bench, underneath a beautiful shade tree, is a comfortable spot for a person to sit and reflect about a latticework of mental models, next to the man who so passionately advocated the value of a liberal arts education.

The 37th Street walkway is a major thoroughfare on the Penn campus. Each morning when class is in session, students spill out of the dormitory building called The Quadrangle and head uphill on 37th. When they reach the intersection with Locust Walk, they splinter off into separate groups, each group heading in a different direction toward the classes in their chosen discipline.

The physics majors turn right and head over to the David Rittenhouse Laboratory on 33rd Street. Biology majors turn left and walk to the Leidy Laboratories on University Avenue. Sociology majors turn left for the Sociology Building located on Locust Walk. Economics majors also turn left and head into the McNeil Building. Political science majors continue straight on 37th Street and go into Stiteler Hall. Psychology majors also continue straight ahead on 37th, to the Psychology Building on Walnut Street. Philosophy majors and English majors turn right onto Locust and walk down to Logan Hall.

The finance students at Penn, who study at the famous Wharton School of Business, have the shortest distance to travel. As Ben Franklin watches silently, they turn right at the intersection and walk just a few steps to Steinberg Hall/Diedrich Hall. There they will spend the next four years taking courses titled Monetary Economics, Corporate and International Finance, Security Analysis, Fixed Income Securities, Real Estate, Investment

Management, and Speculative Markets. At the end of the four years, with college degree in hand, most will seek a job in the financial services industry. A few will attend graduate school and earn an M.B.A. degree for intensely studying for two more years what they have already learned in the previous four.

Sitting next to Ben Franklin one spring afternoon, I wondered to myself what opportunities these hard-charging finance students will have when they graduate, and what additional advantages they would receive if they had spent more of their college experience studying other disciplines. With just one course in physics, they would have learned about Newton's principles, thermodynamics, relativity, and quantum mechanics. They might have also been exposed to wave motion, turbulence, and nonlinearity. They might have realized that the same laws that describe the flow of lava at the earth's center or demonstrate how small-scale shifts in plate tectonics cause large earthquakes also govern the forces in financial markets.

Biology majors at Penn spend four years studying molecular biology and evolution, microbiology and genetics, neurobiology, and the biology of invertebrates and vertebrates, as well as botany and plant development. But a finance major who took but one course, Introduction to Biology, would have learned about viruses, bacteria, protozoa, and plants, and would have studied the diversity of adaptation and evolution. From that one course, in one semester, a perceptive student might have recognized that the patterns that exist in biology look very similar to the patterns that occur in companies and markets.

Students at the Wharton School will have spent a great deal of time studying the theory and structure of financial markets, but what additional insights could they have learned by taking

Economic History and Development, Political Analysis and Revolutionary Behavior, Social Work Practice and Changing Bureaucratic Organizations? To be a successful investor, you need not spend four years studying economics, political science, and sociology, but even a few courses in these disciplines would increase the awareness of how various systems organize, operate, fail, and reorganize.

Today there is little debate over the fact that psychology affects investing. How much value-added benefit to their education would finance students derive from some basic courses in psychology? Perhaps a class on perception and learning: would it be useful to know how a person acquires knowledge and how experience affects behavior? Or cognitive psychology: would it be valuable to understand the mental processes in humans, including how people use pattern recognition to determine action? Even a basic course in abnormal psychology would help a finance major distinguish between normal and abnormal behavior and how different behaviors affect lifestyle.

To work in finance, which is a job about making decisions, how could finance majors pass up courses in modern philosophy, logic, and critical thinking? What mental tools might they acquire by studying the theories of knowledge, mind, and reality expressed by Descartes, Kant, Hegel, James, Wittgenstein, and Dewey? Think of the competitive advantages they could gain from a course on critical thinking, which would give them techniques for analyzing arguments in both natural and statistical language. And finally, what wonderful insights would the finance students have collected had they read only a few of the great books offered in any one of the forty-nine literature courses available for English majors?

Watching the students pass one by one on their way to classes in their chosen major, I can't help but wonder where they will all be in fifty years. Will their college education have adequately prepared them to compete at the highest level? Once they reach retirement age, will they be able to look back and measure their life's work as a success or will they see it as something less than that?

These are the same questions Charlie Munger asked his classmates at the fiftieth reunion of the Harvard Law School class of 1948.[4] "Was our education sufficiently multidisciplinary?" he asked. "In the last fifty years, how far has elite academia progressed toward attainable best-form multidisciplinarity?" To make his point about single-focus thinking, Charlie often employs the proverb "To a man with only a hammer, every problem looks pretty much like a nail." Now, said Charlie, "One partial cure for man-with-hammer tendency is obvious: if a man has a vast set of skills over multidisciplines, he, by definition, carries multiple tools and therefore will limit bad cognitive effects from the 'man with a hammer' tendency. If 'A' is narrow professional doctrine and 'B' consists of the big, extra-useful concepts from other disciplines, then, clearly, the professional possessing 'A' plus 'B' will usually be better off than the poor possessor of 'A' alone. How could it be otherwise?"

Charlie believes that the broad-scale problems we as a society face can be solved only by placing them on a latticework that spreads across many academic disciplines. Therefore, he argues, educational institutions should raise the fluency of a multidisciplinary education. Admittedly, Charlie is quick to add, "we don't have to raise everyone's skill in celestial mechanics to that of Laplace and also ask everyone to achieve a similar level in all other knowledge." Remember, he said, "it turns out that the truly big ideas in each discipline, learned only in essence, carry most of the freight." Furthermore, he continued, to attain broad multidisciplinary skills does not require us to lengthen the already expensive commitment to a college education. "We all know of individuals, modern Ben Franklins, who have achieved a massive multidisciplinary synthesis with less time in formal education than is now available to our numerous brilliant young and thus become better performers in their own disciplines, not worse, despite diversion of learning time to matters outside the normal coverage of their own disciplines." It is Charlie's belief that society would be better off if more college courses across a broader spectrum were made mandatory rather than elective.

● ■ ●

SO AS WE NEAR THE END OF THIS BOOK, we find we have come back full circle to its beginning. The challenge we face as investors and very much as individuals has less to do with the knowledge that is available than with how we choose to put the knowledge pieces together. Similarly, the main problem in education revolves around assembling the pieces of the curriculum. "The ongoing fragmentation of knowledge and resulting chaos are not reflections of the real world but artifacts of scholarship," explains Edward O. Wilson in *Consilience: The Unity of Knowledge.*[5] Consilience, which Wilson describes as the "jumping together" of knowledge from various disciplines, is the only way to create a common framework of explanation.

One of the principal goals of this book is to give you a broader explanation of how markets behave and in the process help you make better investment decisions. One thing we have learned thus far is that our failures to explain are caused by our failures to describe. At the Santa Fe seminar, this notion was articulated frequently by Benoit Mandlebrot, the famed Yale mathematician and father of fractal geometry. If we cannot accurately describe a phenomenon, it is fairly certain we will not be able to accurately explain it. The lesson we are taking away from this book is that the descriptions based solely on finance theories are not enough to explain the behavior of markets.

THE ART OF ACHIEVING what Charlie Munger calls "worldly wisdom" is a pursuit that appears to have more in common with the ancient and medieval periods than with contemporary studies, which mostly emphasize gaining specific knowledge in one particular field. No one would disagree that over the years we have increased our baskets of knowledge, but what is surely missing today is wisdom. Our institutions of higher learning may separate knowledge into categories, but wisdom is what unites them.

Those who make the effort to acquire worldly wisdom are beneficiaries of a special gift. Scientists at Santa Fe call it emergence. Charlie Munger calls it the lollapalooza effect: the extra turbocharge that comes when basic concepts combine and move in the same direction, reinforcing each other's fundamental truths. But whatever you decide to call it, this broad-based understanding is the foundation of worldly wisdom.

The Roman poet Lucretius writes:

> Nothing is more sweet than full possession
> Of those calm heights, well built, well fortified
> By wise men's teaching, to look down from here
> At others wandering below, men lost,
> Confused, in hectic search for the right road.

For many, many people, the financial markets are confusing, and investing has become a hectic search for the right road. But traveling ever more quickly down well-worn roads is not the answer. Rather, looking down from the calm heights of knowledge gained from wise men's teaching is. Those who constantly scan in all directions for what can help them make good decisions will be the successful investors of the future.

SEATED ON THE CAMPUS PARK BENCH, Ben Franklin and I watch as the last of the finance students, now late for class, rush past us. I can't help wonder if he too is thinking about their education and their future. Does he wonder if they have read broadly enough to develop "the connected idea of human affairs" he so eloquently advocated in his 1749 pamphlet? If they have begun to cultivate the habits of mind that will permit them to make connections and link ideas? If they are set on a course of lifelong learning?

He must be thinking about these things, for I think I can hear him quietly read aloud the headline on the *Gazette* he is holding: "The good education of youth has been esteemed by wise men in all ages as the sweet foundation of happiness." It is a simple formula for personal and societal success, as valid today as it was 250 years ago. It is also a timeless road map for achieving worldly wisdom.

NOTES

CHAPTER 1

1. Charles Munger's complete presentation to Dr. Babcock's class, in lightly edited form, appears in the May 5, 1995, edition of *Outstanding Investor Digest [OID]*, from which the quoted passages here are taken. Along with OID editor Henri Emerson, I highly recommend this article be read and reread by all investors.

2. Benjamin Franklin, "Proposals Relating to the Education of Youth in Pensilvania," 1749. All the quotes from Franklin in this section of the chapter are taken from this pamphlet, with his original spelling intact.

3. Professor Richard Beeman, Dean of the College of Arts and Sciences, University of Pennsylvania, interview by author, 23 December, 1999.

4. George Latkoff and Mark Johnson, *Metaphors We Live By* (Chicago: University of Chicago Press, 1980), p. 3.

5. Munger's remarks to the Stanford class and his answers to questions from students appear in two issues of *Outstanding Investor Digest*, 29 December 1997 and 13 March 1998. Again, readers are encouraged to read the lecture, which *OID* editor Henri Emerson aptly describes as "Worldly Wisdom Revisited," in its entirety.

CHAPTER 2

1. Newton's first law of motion states that a moving object will continue moving in a straight line at a constant speed, and a station-

ary object will remain at rest, unless acted on by an unbalanced force; this is the law of inertia. The second law states that the acceleration produced on a body by a force is proportional to the magnitude of the force and inversely proportional to the mass of the object. The third law states that for every action there is an equal and opposite reaction.

2. Alfred Marshall, *Principles of Economics,* 8th ed. (Philadelphia: Porcupine Press, 1920), p. 276.

3. Marshall, *Principles,* p. 269.

4. Marshall, *Principles,* p. 287.

5. Marshall, *Principles,* p. 288.

6. Quoted in Peter Bernstein, *Capital Ideas: The Improbable Origins of Modern Wall Street* (New York: Free Press, 1992), p. 113.

7. Quoted in Bernstein, *Capital Ideas,* p. 37.

8. Quoted in Bernstein, *Capital Ideas,* p. 21.

9. Paul Samuelson, "Proof That Properly Anticipated Prices Fluctuate Randomly," *Industrial Management Review* 6 (Spring 1965).

10. William F. Sharpe, "Capital Asset Prices: A Theory of Market Equilibrium under Conditions of Risk," *Journal of Finance* 19, no. 3 (summer 1964): p. 436.

11. Brian Arthur and others, "Asset Pricing under Endogenous Expectations in an Artificial Stock Market," working paper, Santa Fe Institute Economics Research Program, 96-12-093, 1996.

12. Andrew Lo and Craig MacKinlay, *A Non-Random Walk down Wall Street* (Princeton, N.J.: Princeton University Press, 1999), p. 185.

CHAPTER 3

1. Erasmus Darwin, a prominent and highly successful doctor, was also a poet. It was in his poetry, principally "Zoönomia," that he chose to express his speculations about evolution, in which

he was decidedly ahead of his time. His contemporary, Samuel Taylor Coleridge, took to calling his friend's theories "darwinizing." Although in later years Charles Darwin would claim he was not particularly influenced by his grandfather's theories, it seems impossible that he was unaware of them.

2. *Autobiography of Charles Darwin.*

3. For all that Charles Darwin was able to accomplish, he was not able to explain how variations in species occurred. That question was settled by Gregor Johann Mendel, an Austrian botanist and plant experimenter, who was the first to present a mathematical foundation of the science of genetics. Today, biologists understand that variations within a species are caused by the variations of the genes of its individual members.

4. Richard Dawkins, "International Books of the Year and the Millennium," *Times Literary Supplement,* 3 December 1999.

5. It is interesting to note that a biological view of the economy did not escape the attention of the great economist Alfred Marshall. In the preface to the eighth edition of his famous textbook, *Principles of Economics,* Marshall writes, "The Mecca of the economist lies in economic biology rather than in economic dynamics. But biological conceptions are more complex than those of mechanics; [we] must therefore give a relatively large place to mechanical analogies" (1920, p. xii). What Marshall is saying is that in the 1920s, when the eighth edition was published, it would have been extremely difficult, because of the complexity of experimentation and statistical measurement, to advance knowledge of a biological marketplace. To make any progress at all, it was necessary to idealize a mechanical system that was measurable. But this is now changing. With the advent of the computer, scientists were able to perform the multiple calculations required of a complex system.

6. In an intriguing bit of serendipity, the conference, many months in the planning, was held in 1987, the same year as the stock

market debacle that caused many people to question the concept of absolute equilibrium in the market.

7. J. Doyne Farmer, "Market Force, Ecology, and Evolution," working paper, version 4.1, Santa Fe Institute, 14 February 2000.

8. Farmer, "Market Force," pp. 1, 34.

9. J. Doyne Farmer and Andrew W. Lo, "Frontiers of Finance: Evolution and Efficient Markets," working paper 99-06-039, Santa Fe Institute, 11 April 1999.

10. Jane Jacobs, *The Nature of Economies* (New York: Modern Library, 2000), p. 137.

CHAPTER 4

1. Norman Johnson, S. Ramsussed, and M. Kantor, "The Symbiotic Intelligence Project: Self-Organizing Knowledge on Distributed Networks Drive by Human Interaction," Los Alamos National Laboratory, LA-UR-98-1150, 1998.

2. Marco Dorigo, Gianni Di Caro, and Luca M. Gambardella, "Ant Algorithm for Discrete Optimization," *Artificial Life* 5, no. 3 (1999), pp. 137–172.

3. We have observed anecdotal evidence of emergent behavior before, perhaps without realizing what we were seeing. The recent bestseller *Blind Man's Bluff: The Untold Story of American Submarine Espionage,* by Sherry Sontag and Christopher Drew, presents a very compelling example of emergence. Early in the book, the authors relate the story of the 1966 crash of a B-52 carrying four atomic bombs. Three of the four bombs were soon recovered, but a fourth remained missing, with the Soviets quickly closing in. A naval engineer named John Craven was given the task of locating the missing bomb. He constructed several different scenarios of what possibly could have happened to the fourth bomb and asked the members of his salvage team to wager a bet on where they thought the bomb could be. He then ran each possible location through a computer formula and—

without ever going to sea—was able to pinpoint the exact location of the bomb based on a collective solution.

4. Per Bak, M. Paczuski, and M. Shubik, "Price Variations in a Stock Market with Many Agents," working paper 96-09-078, Santa Fe Institute Economics Research Program, 996.

5. Diana Richards, B. McKay, and W. Richards, "Collective Choice and Mutual Knowledge Structures," *Advanced Complex Systems* 1 (1998), pp. 221–236.

CHAPTER 5

1. Charles Ellis, "A Conversation with Benjamin Graham," *Financial Analysts Journal* (September/October 1976) p. 20.

2. Charles Ellis, a series of interviews by author, 1993–1994.

3. Benjamin Graham and David Dodd, *Security Analysis* (New York: McGraw-Hill, 1951), p. 38.

4. John Maynard Keynes, *The General Theory of Employment, Interest, and Money* (New York: Harcourt Brace, 1964).

5. Benjamin Graham, *The Intelligent Investor* (New York: Harper & Row, 1973), p. 3.

6. As quoted in Ellis, "Conversation," p. 20.

7. Brad Barber and Terrance Odean, "The Courage of Misguided Convictions," *Financial Analysts Journal* (November/December 1999).

8. In 1997, Terrance Odean, professor of finance at the University of California, analyzed ten thousand randomly selected accounts from a major discount brokerage firm, comparing them to market averages over several periods. Among his findings: these investors sold and repurchased 78 percent of their portfolio each year, with disastrous results—the stocks these investors bought consistently trailed the market and the ones they sold actually beat the market (Barber and Odean, "Misguided Convictions"). For more on this, also see Fuerbringer, "Why Both Bulls and Bears Can Act So Bird Brained," *New York Times,* 30 March 1997, Sect. 3, p. 6.

9. In this respect, the phrase "mental models" as used here is more specific than Charlie Munger's use of the same phrase; his meaning is closer to "key principle, core idea" than to a sense of dimensional representation.

10. Kenneth Craik, *The Nature of Explanation* (London: Cambridge University Press, 1952).

11. Michael Shermer, *How We Believe* (New York: W. H. Freeman, 2000), p. 36.

12. Quoted in Peter Bernstein, *Capital Ideas*, p. 124.

13. Claude E. Shannon, "A Mathematical Theory of Communication," *The Bell Systems Technical* (July 1948).

CHAPTER 6

1. Lee McIntyre, "Complexity: A Philosopher's Reflections," *Complexity* 3, no. 6 (1998), p. 26.

2. McIntyre, "Complexity," p. 27.

3. McIntyre, "Complexity," p. 28.

4. Charles S. Peirce, "How to Make Our Ideas Clear," *Popular Science Monthly* (January 1878). Also in Louis Menand (ed.), *Pragmatism: A Reader* (New York: Random House, 1997), p. 26.

5. William James, "Pragmatism: Conception of Truth," Lecture VI in *Pragmatism* (originally published 1907, reprinted 1995; New York: Dover Publications, 1995), p. 30.

6. James, *Pragmatism*, p. 22.

7. James, *Pragmatism*, p. 23.

8. James, *Pragmatism*, p. 24.

9. James, *Pragmatism*, p. 26.

10. James, *Pragmatism*, p. 31.

11. Jeffery M. Laderman, "Value Investing Learns New Tricks," *Business Week*, 14 June 1999, p. 128.

12. Jim Rapper, "Fund Phenom, Bill Miller's Silent Advisors: Peirce, Dewey, & James," *Washington and Lee Alumni Magazine*, fall 1999, p. 25.

13. Diane Baregas, "Natural Fund Manager, Bill Miller Sees Value in Business Network," *SFI Bulletin,* winter 1998, p. 13.

14. For a review of this classic argument, see the exchange between Bill Miller and James Cramer in Robert Hagstrom, *The Warren Buffett Portfolio* (New York: Wiley, 1999), pp. 101–104.

15. Correct use of the dividend discount model requires us to make difficult calculations. What will be the future growth rate of the company over its lifetime? How much cash will the company generate? What is the appropriate discount rate for projecting the growth of cash flows? Answers to these tough questions are the necessary input variables for the dividend-discount model. Adding to the difficulty is the fear that the uncertainty of long-range forecasts makes using the model suspect. A further difficulty is that determining value is highly sensitive to its initial condition; even a slight change in growth rate or the discount factor can have a large effect on value. For this reason, investors often use shortcuts (second-order models) to determine value.

16. James, *Pragmatism,* p. 24.

17. Baregas, "Natural Fund Manager," p. 14.

18. Rapper, "Fund Phenom," p. 27.

CHAPTER 7

1. A number of other institutions of higher learning have special liberal arts programs grounded in the works of history's greatest thinkers. Some are part of the university's honors program; others are short-term intensive-study programs. St. John's is the only university I am aware of that is exclusively dedicated to teaching the "great books"; its list of curriculum materials is continuously reviewed and updated.

2. Indeed, St. John's dates back to 1696, five years before Yale was founded, fifty years before Princeton, and sixty-three years before Franklin's famous education manifesto.

3. Don Bell, Goldman Sachs (St. John's, class of 1992), and Lee Munson, Prime Charter Ltd. (class of 1997), interview by author 7 June 2000; Warren Spector, Bear Stearns & Co. (class of 1981), interview by author 14 June 2000.

4. Mortimer Adler served as editor of the fifty-four-volume *Great Books of the Western World* and as chairman of *Encyclopaedia Britannica*'s board of editors for twenty years. Today he is, at ninety-seven, still actively writing and speaking on his lifelong passion: the value of a broad general education based in the humanities.

5. Few reference works in any discipline have the staying power of *How to Read a Book*. The copy I own is from the thirty-sixth printing of the revised edition.

6. Mortimer Adler and Charles van Doren, *How to Read a Book*, rev. ed. (New York: Simon & Schuster, 1972), pp. 46–47.

7. Adler and van Doren, p. 19.

8. Adler and van Doren, p. 291.

9. Adler and van Doren, p. 301.

10. Adler and van Doren, p. 205.

11. Charlie Munger, 1996 address at Stanford Law School, reprinted in *Outstanding Investor Digest*, 13 March 1998, p. 58.

12. Munger, pp. 63, 61.

CHAPTER 8

1. The seminar "Beyond Equilibrium and Efficiency" was held at the Santa Fe Institute, Santa Fe, New Mexico, 18–21 May 2000. All comments and quotes from the participants presented in this chapter were noted by the author, who was in attendance.

2. The logic of looking for the keys where the light is was argued with particular eloquence by mathematician David Weinberger, senior adviser at O'Connor Partners, USB Warburg.

3. I am indebted to John Holland, professor of psychology and engineering and computer sciences at the University of Michigan, for his graceful presentation of the concepts of building blocks, the need for models that are dynamic, and the flight simulator analogy.

4. Charles T. Munger, "The Need for More Multidisciplinary Skill," presented May 1998, at the 50th Reunion of the Harvard Law School Class Graduated in 1948. The full text of the speech appears in Appendix B of Janet Lowe's book *Damn Right: Behind the Scenes with Berkshire Hathaway Billionaire Charlie Munger* (New York: John Wiley & Sons, 2000).

5. Edward O. Wilson, *Consilience: The Unity of Knowledge* (New York: Vintage Books, 1999), p. 8.

READING LIST

CHAPTER 1

Bell, Daniel. *The Reforming of General Education.* New York: Columbia University Press, 1966.

Birkhoff, Garrett. *Lattice Theory.* Providence, R.I.: American Mathematical Society, 1979.

Black, Max. *Models and Metaphors: Studies in Language and Philosophy,* rev. ed. Ithaca, N.Y.: Cornell University Press, 1966.

Burke, James. *Connections.* Boston: Little, Brown, 1978.

Farmer, J. Doyne. "A Rosetta Stone for Connectionism," *Physica D,* vol. 42 (1990).

Franklin, Benjamin. *Autobiography.* Numerous editions of Franklin's fascinating work are available today.

Holland, John H. *Emergence: From Chaos to Emergence.* Reading, Mass.: Helix Books, a division of Addison-Wesley, 1998.

Holland, John H. *Hidden Order: How Adaptation Builds Complexity.* Reading, Mass.: Addison-Wesley, 1995.

Lakoff, George, and Johnson, Mark. *Metaphors We Live By.* Chicago: University of Chicago Press, 1980.

Locke, John. "Some Thoughts Concerning Education." 1693.

Lucas, Christopher. *Crisis in the Academy: Rethinking American Higher Education in America.* New York: St. Martin's, 1998.

Milton, John. "Of Education." 1644.

Van Doren, Carl. *Benjamin Franklin.* This Pulitzer Prize–winning biography of Franklin, originally written in 1934, has been produced in numerous editions by several publishers.

Wilson, Edward O. *Consilience: The Unity of Knowledge.* New York: Alfred A. Knopf, 1998.

CHAPTER 2

Anderson, Philip W., Arrow, Kenneth J., and Pines, David, eds. *The Economy as an Evolving Complex System.* Reading, Mass.: Perseus Books, 1988.

Arthur, Brian W., Durlauf, Steven N., and Lane, David A., eds. *The Economy as an Evolving Complex System II.* Reading, Mass.: Addison-Wesley, 1997.

Arthur, Brian, and others. "Asset Pricing under Endogenous Expectations in an Artificial Stock Market." Working Paper for SFI Economics Research Program, 96-12-093, 1996.

Bak, Per, Paczuski, M., and Subik, M. "Price Variations in a Stock Market with Many Agents." Working paper for SFI Economics Research Program, 96-09-075, 1996.

Bernstein, Peter L. *Capital Ideas: The Improbable Origins of Modern Wall Street.* New York: The Free Press, 1992.

Bronowski, Jacob. *The Ascent of Man.* Boston: Little, Brown, 1973.

Fama, Eugene. "Efficient Capital Markets: A Review of Theory and Empirical Work." *Journal of Finance,* May 1970, vol. 25, no. 2.

Farmer, J. Doyne. "Physicists Attempt to Scale the Ivory Towers of Finance." Working paper for SFI Economics Research Program, 99-10-073, 1999.

Farmer, J. Doyne, and Lo, Andrew. "Frontier of Finance: Evolution and Efficient Markets." Working paper for SFI Economics Research Program, 99-06-039, 1999.

Focardi, Sergio. "From Equilibrium to Non-Linear Dynamics in Investment Management." *Journal of Portfolio Management,* summer 1996.

Gleick, James. *Chaos: Making a New Science.* New York: Penguin Books, 1987.

Hagstrom, Robert G. *The Warren Buffett Portfolio: Mastering the*

Power of the Focus Investment Strategy. New York: John Wiley & Sons, 1999.

Lo, Andrew W., and MacKinlay, Craig A. *A Non-Random Walk down Wall Street.* Princeton, N.J.: Princeton University Press, 1999.

Mantegna, Rosario, and Stanley, Eugene H. *An Introduction to Econophysics: Correlations and Complexity in Finance.* Cambridge, England: Cambridge University Press, 2000.

Marshall, Alfred. *Principles of Economics,* 8th ed. Philadelphia: Porcupine Press, 1920.

Nicolis, Gregoire, and Prigogine, Ilya. *Exploring Complexity: An Introduction.* New York: W. H. Freeman, 1989.

Samuelson, Paul A. "Proof That Properly Anticipated Prices Fluctuate Randomly." *Industrial Management Review* 6, spring 1965.

Samuelson, Paul A., and Nordhaus, William D. *Economics,* 12th ed. New York: McGraw-Hill, 1985.

Sharpe, William F. "Capital Asset Prices: A Theory of Market Equilibrium under Conditions of Risk." *Journal of Finance,* summer 1964, vol. 19, no. 3.

Strathern, Paul. *The Big Idea: Newton and Gravity.* New York: Doubleday, 1997.

Trefil, James, and Hazen, Robert M. *The Sciences: An Integrated Approach.* New York: John Wiley & Sons, 2000.

Westfall, Richard S. *The Life of Isaac Newton.* New York: Cambridge University Press, 1994.

Wilson, Edward O. *Consilience: The Unity of Knowledge.* New York: Vintage Books, 1998.

Zimmerman, Brenda, Lindberg, Curt, and Plsek, Paul. *Edgeware: Insights from Complexity Science for Health Care Leaders.* Irving, Texas: VHA, Inc., 1998.

CHAPTER 3

Colinvaux, Paul. *Why Big Fierce Animals Are Rare.* Princeton, N.J.: Princeton University Press, 1978.

Christensen, Clayton. *The Innovators' Dilemma*. Boston: Harvard Business School Press, 1997.

Darwin, Charles. *Voyage of the* Beagle. London: Penguin Books, 1989 (reprint).

Darwin, Charles. *The Origin of Species*. New York: Gramercy Books, 1979 (reprint).

Darwin, Francis, ed. *The Autobiography of Charles Darwin*. New York: Dover Publications, 1958 (reprint). (Originally published in 1893 as *Charles Darwin, His Life Told in an Autobiographical Chapter and in a Selected Series of His Letters, Edited by His Son*.)

Dawkins, Richard. *The Selfish Gene*. New York: Oxford University Press, 1976.

Dawkins, Richard. *The Blind Watchmaker*. New York: W.W. Norton, 1996.

Dennett, Daniel C. *Darwin's Dangerous Idea*. New York: Simon & Schuster, 1995.

Gould, Stephen Jay. *Dinosaur in a Haystack*. New York: Crown, 1995.

Haeckel, Stephan. *Adaptive Enterprise*. Boston: Harvard Business School Press, 1999.

Jacobs, Jane. *The Nature of Economies*. New York: Modern Library, 2000.

Jones, Steve. *Almost Like a Whale*. London: Doubleday, 1999.

Martel, Leon. *Mastering Change*. New York: Simon & Schuster, 1986.

Mayr, Ernst. *The Growth of Biological Thought*. Cambridge, Mass.: Harvard University Press, 1982.

Ormerod, Paul. *Butterfly Economics*. New York: Pantheon Books, 1998.

Ridley, Mark. *Evolution*. Cambridge, Mass.: Blackwell Science, 1996.

Rothschild, Michael. *Bionomics: Economy as Ecosystem*. New York: Henry Holt, 1990.

Weibull, Jorgen. *Evolutionary Game Theory*. Cambridge, Mass.: The MIT Press, 1995.

CHAPTER 4

Bak, Per. *How Nature Works.* New York: Copernicus, Springer-Verlag, 1996.

Grodon, Deborah. *Ants at Work: How an Insect Society Is Organized.* New York: The Free Press, 1999.

Holldobler, Bert, and Wilson, Edward O. *Journey to the Ants.* Cambridge, Mass.: Harvard University Press, 1994.

Krugman, Paul. *The Self-Organizing Economy.* Malden, Mass.: Blackwell, 1996.

Schweitzer, Frank, ed. *Self-Organization of Complex Structures: From Individuals to Collective Dynamics.* Amsterdam: Gordon and Breach Science Publishers, 1997.

Smith, Adam. *An Inquiry into the Nature and Causes of the Wealth of Nations.* New York: Modern Library, 1937 (reprint); originally published 1776.

Sontag, Sherry, and Drew, Christopher. *Blind Man's Bluff: The Story of American Submarine Espionage.* New York: Public Affairs, 1998.

Sumner, William Graham. *Social Darwinism: Selected Essays.* Englewood Cliffs, N.J.: Prentice-Hall, 1963.

Wilson, Edward O. *In Search of Nature.* Washington, D.C.: Island Press, 1996.

CHAPTER 5

Belsky, Gary, and Gilovich, Thomas. *Why Smart People Make Big Money Mistakes.* New York: Simon & Schuster, 1999.

Bernstein, Peter L. *Capital Ideas: The Improbable Origins of Modern Wall Street.* New York: The Free Press, 1992.

Chancellor, Edward. *Devil Take the Hindmost.* New York: Farrar Strauss & Giroux, 1999.

Cialdini, Robert B. *Influence: The Psychology of Persuasion.* New York: William Morrow, 1993.

Craik, Kenneth. *The Nature of Explanation.* London: Cambridge University Press, 1952 (originally published 1943).

De La Vega, Joseph. *Confusion de Confusiones*. New York: John Wiley & Sons, 1996.

Gilovich, Thomas. *How We Know What Isn't So*. New York: The Free Press, 1991.

Graham, Benjamin, and Dodd, David. *Security Analysis*. New York: McGraw-Hill, 1951; originally published 1934.

Graham, Benjamin. *The Intelligent Investor*. New York: Harper & Row, 1973; originally published 1949.

Hagstrom, Robert. *The Warren Buffett Portfolio*. New York: John Wiley & Sons, 1999.

Johnson-Laird, Philip N. *Mental Models*. Cambridge, Mass.: Harvard University Press, 1983.

Kahneman, Daniel, Slovic, Paul, and Tversky, Amos. *Judgement under Uncertainty: Heuristic and Biases*. Cambridge: Cambridge University Press, 1982.

Kindleberger, Charles P. *Manias, Panics, and Crashes*. New York: John Wiley & Sons, 1996.

Le Bon, Gustave. *The Crowd*. New York: Penguin Books, reprint edition 1977; originally published 1895.

Lowe, Janet. *Ben Graham on Value Investing*. Chicago: Dearborn Financial Publishing, 1994.

Mackay, Charles. *Extraordinary Popular Delusions and the Madness of Crowds*. New York: John Wiley & Sons, reprint 1996; originally published 1841.

Shefrin, Hersh. *Beyond Fear and Greed*. Boston, Mass.: Harvard University Press, 2000.

Sherden, William A. *The Fortune Sellers*. New York: John Wiley & Sons, 1998.

Shermer, Michael. *How We Believe*. New York: W.H. Freeman, 2000.

Shermer, Michael. *Why People Believe Weird Things*. New York: W.H. Freeman, 1977.

Shiller, Robert J. *Irrational Exuberance*. Princeton, N.J.: Princeton University Press, 2000

Shiller, Robert J. *Market Volatility*. Cambridge, Mass.: The MIT Press, 1997.

Thaler, Richard H. *The Winners' Curse*. Princeton, N.J.: Princeton University Press, 1992.

Tvede, Lars. *The Psychology of Finance*. New York: John Wiley & Sons, 1999.

CHAPTER 6

Audi, Robert. *The Cambridge Dictionary of Philosophy*. Cambridge: Cambridge University Press, 1995.

De Botton, Alain. *The Consolations of Philosophy*. New York: Pantheon Books, 2000.

Dickstein, Morris. *The Revival of Pragmatism: New Essays on Thought, Law, and Culture*. Durham and London: Duke University Press, 1998.

Honderich, Ted, ed. *The Oxford Companion to Philosophy*. Oxford: Oxford University Press, 1995.

James, William. *Pragmatism*. New York: Dover Publications, 1995.

Menand, Louis, ed. *Pragmatism: A Reader*. New York: Random House, 1997.

Simon, Linda. *Genuine Reality: A Life of William James*. New York: Harcourt, Brace, 1998.

White, Morton. *Pragmatism and the American Mind*. New York: Oxford University Press, 1973.

CHAPTER 7

Adler, Mortimer J. *How to Speak, How to Listen*. New York: Simon & Schuster, 1983.

Adler, Mortimer J., and Van Doren, Charles. *How to Read a Book*, rev. ed. New York: Simon & Schuster, 1972.

Bloom, Harold. *The Western Canon: The Books and Schools for the Ages,* New York: Riverhead Books, 1994.

Bloom, Harold. *How to Read and Why*. New York: Scribners, 2000.

Woolf, Virginia. *The Common Reader: The First Series*. Edited and introduced by Andrew McNeillie. New York: Harcourt Brace Jovanovich, 1984; originally published 1925.

Woolf, Virginia. *The Common Reader: The Second Series*. Edited and introduced by Andrew McNeillie. New York: Harcourt Brace Jovanovich, 1986; originally published 1932.

ACKNOWLEDGMENTS

You would not be holding this book were it not for the writing talent and editorial direction of my writing partner, Maggie Stuckey, for the old cliché is literally true: I could not have written it without her. This is the fourth book Maggie and I have written together, and I can honestly say that her skills have never shone more brightly. As I mentioned in the preface, this was a particularly hard book to write, but Maggie never shied away from the challenge. Although we work at opposite ends of the country, I have always been impressed with her ability to instantly connect with the material and to know exactly what I want to say even before I can verbalize it. In this book I came to rely on her to magically find the one additional fact that clarifies a complex theory, the one historical tidbit that makes a story come alive, or the one perfect way to say what I had become entangled in trying to explain. I as the author and you as the reader are very fortunate that Maggie Stuckey has willingly shared her natural gifts with us.

I also wish to thank David Pendlebury, research manager at the Institute for Scientific Information, for carefully reading the entire manuscript and offering countless suggestions for improving the book.

Several others have read portions of the book, have shared their valuable time discussing some of its topics, or both. At the

University of Pennsylvania I would like to thank Richard Beeman, Paul Sniegowski, and Larry Gladney. Also at the university, I'd like to thank William Wunner, director of biotechnology at The Wistar Institute. All the members of the Santa Fe Institute have been very giving with their thoughts and suggestions. I am particularly grateful to Doyne Farmer and Brian Arthur for their willingness to patiently teach me new ideas. At the Los Alamos National Laboratory I would like to thank Norman Johnson for sharing his research on the Symbiotic Intelligence Project.

A special thanks to Charlie Munger for his earliest words of encouragement and for planting the original idea for this book. Thanks also to Michael Mauboussin, U.S. Equity Strategist at CS First Boston, for his continuing discussions about mental models, and to Bob Coleman at Gardner Russo Gardner for his thoughtful comments and support.

I am greatly indebted to Laurie Harper at Sebastian Agency. Laurie is a splendid agent who manages to navigate the world of publishing with great integrity. Her professionalism, her forthright honesty, and her warm humor are greatly appreciated.

It has been a wonderful experience to become a part of TEXERE Publishing. A warm congratulation to Myles Thompson and his wonderful team for everything they have accomplished. Thanks also to Jena Pincott for her thoughtful editorial suggestions.

Writing is both challenging and time-consuming. Nowhere does its effect weigh more heavily than on the author's family. For her unwavering support, I owe more than I can possibly say to my wife, Maggie. Her love makes everything possible.

I am very fortunate to be a part of Legg Mason Funds Management, Inc. It is an extraordinary group of people. The portfolio managers, analysts, traders, and support staff have all generously provided intellectual support for this project, and I am deeply grateful. A very special thank-you to Ericka Peterson and Cathy Coladonato for their hard work and dedication at Focus Capital.

Lastly, I owe a lifetime of thanks to Bill Miller, whose intellectual generosity is unmatched. Thank you, Bill, for introducing me to the Santa Fe Institute, to the writings of the great Argentine writer Jorge Luis Borges, and to the philosophy of pragmatism.

For all that is good and right about this book, you may thank the people I have mentioned here. For any errors and omissions, I alone am responsible.

INDEX